MW01490243

Becoming
Eating Your Way to Bountiful Health

Discovering joy, freedom, and fulfillment in choosing foods that bring life to your body

Christy Wade

Victorious Living
Publishing House
Wendell, NC

Published by:
Victorious Living Publishing House
1104 Sandrock Lane
Wendell, NC 27591

The purpose of this book is to provide information regarding nutrition and its role in the health of our physical bodies. It is in no way intended to be a medical manual, or to take the place of medical advice from a licensed practitioner. Because of inherent risks associated with changes in diet, the author assumes neither responsibility nor liability for any adverse effects resulting directly or indirectly from the application of the information presented in this book. Readers should consult a qualified health professional with regard to any medical conditions or prescribed medications. You have the constitutional right to make decisions regarding treatment of your personal health conditions, but the author and publisher take no responsibility for any injury, loss, or damage to any person who reads or follows the information presented in this book.

NIV Scripture taken from the Holy Bible New International Version, copyright © 1973, 1978, 1984 by International Bible Society.

Clip art used with permission – ©2005 www.Clip art.com

Publisher's Cataloging-in-Publication Data

Wade, Christy.
  Becoming Whole : Eating Your Way to Bountiful
Health — Second Edition / Christy Wade.
    p. cm.

ISBN 0-9766256-2-8

Library of Congress Control Number: 2006922962

10 9 8 7 6 5 4 3 2 1

*Dedicated to my children:
Lindsey, Dylan, Joshua, and Rachel. May
you always seek wisdom and truth, and
love the Lord with all your heart, mind,
soul, and strength.*

Acknowledgments

To those in my life who have supported me on this project, I am forever grateful. Thank you to my husband Mike for your patience and support, and to our children Lindsey, Dylan, Joshua, and Rachel, for your continuous prayers and encouraging words. Thank you to my many friends who continually encouraged me to press on and complete this project.

Special thanks go to those who have had their hand in the editing and refining process. Dale and Teresa, what would this book be without you? Words are not adequate to express my appreciation for your creative thoughts, ideas, and hours spent working with me. Thank you, Cher, for sharing your wit and wisdom, creativity, encouragement, and your zest for life. Thanks also to Lisa, Donna, Debbie, Jeannie, Christine, Mary Nell, and Charles for the many hours you spent laboring over this book.

Above all I thank God for His kindness and mercy in leading me on the path to good health, for the gift of wonderful family and friends, and for His Spirit which is ever present. Certainly I could not have written this book without His continual guidance and strength, and the wisdom and insights found in His Word. Thank you, Jesus, for your faithfulness!

Table of Contents

Preface

Congratulations! You hold in your hands a book that can physically and spiritually change your life forever! Are you looking for better health, weight loss, more energy, and freedom from sickness and disease? Do you believe you can achieve good health in your physical body and enjoy it? Do you know that your body is a temple of the Holy Spirit, and that God created it to glorify Himself? Are you glorifying God in your physical body as well as in your spirit? Will you be able to continue to do so in the future, based on your current lifestyle?

This book was created for use as an individual or group study. It gives you the knowledge base, practical tips, and encouragement you need to embrace a healthy lifestyle. Whether you choose to complete this study with a group or by yourself, I pray that God will speak to you through His Word, and that you will continue to seek Him in all areas of your life, including your physical health.

You are now beginning a very exciting journey, one in which you will discover many truths that could change your life. Come along and enjoy the beautiful scenery, the good company, and a new level of health and vitality as we travel along the road to good health together!

Taste and see that the Lord is good.
Psalm 34:8a

Introduction

Do you know anyone who has set out in life with the intention of getting sick? Most of us are more likely to pray for health, do what we've learned to do (sometimes!) and hope for the best. Yet Americans are dying of disease more often than from any other cause, and Christians are no different than unbelievers in this regard. We suffer from the same illnesses and diseases as unbelievers, and we die at the same rate as unbelievers from these same causes. If our God is a healing God … and He is … how can this be? Aren't we called to be the *"salt of the earth"* (Matthew 5:13), the *"light of the world"* (Matthew 5:14), and to *"shine like stars"* (Philippians 2:15)? God has given each of us a purpose in life, and a mission to accomplish. Do *you* have the good health, vitality, and clarity of mind to fulfill God's plan for your life?

Many of us believe that because God is all-powerful, it must be His will when sickness and disease strike. After all, He can choose to heal us if He so desires, but should we expect Him to heal us even when we are eating foods that are detrimental to our physical bodies? We submit ourselves to the Lord in spiritual areas, finance, family, and more, but have we submitted ourselves to the Lord in the area of physical health? God created our bodies to be self-healing, and He knows best how to nourish and care for them. There are foods that cause health and life, and those that cause sickness and death. God has given us *"everything we need for life and godliness"* (2 Peter 1:3). Scripture should be our guidebook to follow in learning to maintain health and vitality.

God created man. Genesis 2:7 says, *"the Lord God formed the man from the dust of the ground and breathed into his nostrils the breath of life, and the man became a living being."* In Psalm 139:13 we read, *"For you created my inmost being; you knit me together in my mother's womb. I praise you because I am fearfully and wonderfully made; your works are wonderful, I know that full well."* Your body is the dwelling place of the Holy Spirit. *"Do you not know that your body is a temple of the Holy Spirit, who is in you, whom you have received from God? You are not your own; you were bought at a price. Therefore honor God with your body"* (1 Corinthians 6:19-20). God desires that we live in good health. 3 John 2 says, *"Dear friend, I pray that you may enjoy good health and that all may go well with you, even as your soul is getting along well."*

For everything that was written in the past was written to teach us, so that through endurance and the encouragement of the Scriptures we might have hope. Romans 15:4

Unfortunately, Christians tend to treat their bodies in many of the same ways as the world does. Many of us have neither the knowledge base to know how to properly care for our bodies to prevent disease, nor any understanding of what is really happening in our bodies when sickness and disease occur. Is God controlling your health if you are feeding your body food it was never designed to handle, and denying your body the food it requires to build healthy cells? How can we expect Him to keep it in perfect working order if in the natural we are doing just the opposite? Can you really say it must be God's will for you to be sick simply because He has not miraculously healed you?

Do you believe that God desires for you to live in good health? Are you overweight, frequently sick, or fearful of diseases so prevalent today such as cancer, heart disease, or diabetes? Most of us would want to maintain a healthy, strong, and vibrant body if we only knew we could do it. We either don't know where to begin, believe we could never maintain it, or have the misconception that leading a healthy lifestyle is difficult and boring.

I have great news for you! You *can* maintain a healthy, vibrant body, and you do not need to be fearful of sickness and disease.

God has created your body to maintain good health and to rid itself of disease when given proper nutrition and care. He truly created an amazing body. The information I will share with you in this book is Scripturally and scientifically sound, but is not common knowledge to most of us. In order to achieve God's results, we must choose His ways.

Learning how to gain and maintain a healthy body, and implementing a healthy lifestyle, is really exciting! Losing weight and watching physical issues that you have dealt with for so long simply disappear is wonderfully magnificent. You will be awestruck at God over the marvelous body He created when you see it in action the way He designed it to be.

Will you join me on this journey to good health? Come along as we learn the key ingredients of healthy living, what Scripture and science have to say about it, and practical advice on how to implement a healthy lifestyle in your family. Join me now, and begin to experience the great freedom that comes from living a life-giving, health-promoting lifestyle.

*For by him all things were created: things in heaven
and on earth, visible and invisible, whether thrones or
powers or rulers or authorities; all things
were created by him and for him.
Colossians 1:16*

Chapter One

Steeped in Tradition—
Time Honored Truth ...
or Fiction?

*See to it that no one takes you captive through hollow
and deceptive philosophy, which depends on
human tradition and the basic principles
of this world rather than on Christ.*
Colossians 2:8

As I walk along the road on my journey to good health, I am amazed at the deception I have been under in so many areas of my life. As Bible believing Christians who seek the Lord and desire to please Him, we hope we know the ways of the Lord and are walking in them. But we live in the world, and often the traditions of men have a way of becoming our lifestyle, even when they are in opposition to God's Word. Jesus said, "You have let go of the commandments of God and are holding onto the traditions of men" (Mark 7:8).

Stop for a moment and reminisce about your family traditions involving food when you were a child. Here are some examples to jump-start your thinking:

◆ Were your meals planned according to the four food groups?

◆ Were social events centered around snacks and meals?

◆ Did you primarily eat whole grains or refined flour? ("Enriched flour" is not a whole grain).

◆ Were certain foods associated with particular days/holidays?

◆ Did your parents drink coffee every morning?

◆ Was dinner incomplete without dessert?

◆ Did you eat until you were "stuffed," and then snack again before the next meal or before going to bed?

What specific traditions involving food did your family have when you were a child? How many of them have you carried into your own family as an adult?

Love the Lord your God with all your heart and with all your soul and with all your strength. Deuteronomy 6:5

My mother is a fantastic cook! To this day, we all love to gather in Mom's kitchen and eat. She lovingly prepared our meals and snacks, and taught us to cook along side of her. I can still picture the scrumptious meals we shared. Our dinner table was really a wonderful family time, with good food, laughs, and sharing our lives together.

We were taught in school which foods were healthy, according to the four food groups, and we based our food choices on that model. We assumed that these foods brought health to our bodies. With my knowledge based on this model, I was under the impression that if I ate a meal with meat, potatoes, bread, salad, a vegetable, and a glass of milk, it was a very healthy meal! By "healthy," I mean that it would cause my body to be in good health and to function properly, without sickness or pain as God designed. That is certainly not the way it was. I suffered with an irritable stomach, psoriasis, and frequent headaches all of my childhood. At the age of nineteen I was diagnosed with colitis, and my headaches grew worse. By the time I was twenty-eight, I had migraines on a regular basis, and had broken out with psoriasis over 90% of my body. Let me tell you, this was not a pretty sight! People were praying for me regularly, and I sought out and accepted prayer at every opportunity. I began to question God about the source of my illness. Surely He didn't intend for me to be sick continually, yet He wasn't healing me. Was there more to being healed than believing in faith for my healing?

God's Word speaks to us in all areas of our lives. He is not silent. Jesus said, *"Ask and it will be given to you; seek and you will find; knock and the door will be opened to you. For everyone who asks receives; he who seeks finds; and to him who knocks, the door will be opened. Which of you, if his son asks for bread, will give him a stone? Or if he asks for a fish, will give him a snake? If you, then, though you are evil, know how to give good gifts to your children, how much more will your Father in heaven give good gifts to those who ask him!"* (Matthew 7:7-11). When we ask, He will answer. God delights in sharing His truth with us!

Whatever the God of heaven has prescribed, let it be done with diligence for the temple of the God of heaven.
Ezra 7:23a

As Christians, we have devoted so much time to the care and well being of our spiritual lives, we have all but neglected our physical bodies. I am not talking about being poorly dressed and underfed. In fact, it's just the opposite. We are often well dressed and  overfed, which is a sure sign of a prosperous nation. We have been blessed with such abundance that we lavish it upon ourselves, almost without thought. When we get tired of carrying around the extra weight we "diet," or when we're fatigued, depressed, or

Thou shouldst eat to live; not live to eat.
Socrates

plagued with illness, we visit the doctor and begin taking medication. Is this the lifestyle that God planned for us, or have we strayed from His perfect plan? *"For I know the plans I have for you," declares the Lord, "plans to prosper you and not to harm you, plans to give you a hope and a future"* (Jeremiah 29:11).

With all of the time we devote to our spiritual health through prayer, studying God's Word, fellowshipping with the saints, and serving in ministry, isn't it time we devote a season to learning about our physical bodies, and how to properly nourish and care for the "temple" God created for Himself? The Bible says we were created body, soul, and spirit. Let's take some time together to focus on health, healing, and the abundant freedom of choosing to live a healthy lifestyle. I hope you enjoy this wonderful journey on the road to good health. It is my prayer that you will be drawn to our Lord Jesus Christ through this study of His Word, and that you will long for Him and delight in His ways. May you never settle for what the world has to offer, but diligently seek the Lord and gladly receive what He delights to give you. In the next few chapters we will unlock some of the riches of God's Word, so you may be abundantly blessed in your body as well as in your spirit.

Chapter 1 Study Questions

1. Write Mark 7:8-9.

    _____

    _____

    _____

2. List three traditions regarding food that your family had when you were a child. Which of these do you still follow?

    _____

    _____

    _____

3. List three food habits that you currently have.

    _____

    _____

    _____

4. What effect do these traditions and habits have on you emotionally? Physically?

    _____

    _____

    _____

5. Do you consider them positive or negative aspects in your life? Why?

_____

_____

_____

6. Write out 1 Corinthians 6:19-20.

_____

_____

7. How much thought and time do you spend each day caring for the health of your physical body?

_____

_____

_____

8. Write your basic belief and understanding of the principles of maintaining a healthy body. Are you currently following these principles?

_____

_____

_____

9. On a scale of 1-10, with 1 being least important and 10 being most important, how would you rate the importance of good health to you and your family?

   _____

10. Describe what the term "good health" means to you.

   _____

   _____

   _____

11. Copy 3 John 2.

   _____

   _____

   _____

12. Consider where you are on this journey to good health. Are you on the road yet, or are you still sitting at the beginning watching others embark on their journeys? Did you begin your journey and wander off the road somewhere, or are you traveling on this road to good health and reaping its benefits?

   _____

   _____

Write a prayer expressing your thoughts to God on your current state of health. Ask the Lord to give you wisdom and insight regarding the care of your physical body, and the desire and motivation to gain and maintain a healthy body. Place the care of your physical body in His hands, just as you do your spirit and other aspects of your life.

_____

_____

_____

_____

_____

_____

_____

Chapter Two

Minced, Mashed, Glazed or Garnished... What's Your Condition?

Jesus said, "If you hold to my teaching,
you are really my disciples.
Then you will know the truth,
and the truth will set you free."
John 8:32

You may be asking, "Free from what?" This passage is first and foremost speaking about the truth of Jesus Christ setting us free from sin and death through His sacrifice on the cross. In order to be free to follow Jesus in every aspect of our lives, we must first let go of our own agenda and ways of doing things. Jesus was speaking to Jews who were so set in their traditions, they didn't recognize that it was Christ who was speaking to them.

We have already been warned not to forsake the commandments of God for the traditions of men (Colossians 2:8), but you might ask, "What is so bad about our family traditions regarding food?" Following is a little quiz that might shed some light on the current condition of your physical body:

- Do you have physical pain in your body on a regular basis (back ache, joint pain, head ache, etc.)?
- Do you sleep well and awaken refreshed, or do you have restless sleep, and awaken tired?
- Are you overweight or struggling to maintain your weight?
- Do you suffer from depression, high cholesterol, reflux disease, or any other conditions for which you are on prescription medication?
- Do you believe you are out of control in the area of eating?
- Do you often eat more than you think you should and feel guilty?
- Do you often eat foods you know are unhealthy for your body?
- Do you go through your day with energy and vigor, or do you drag through the day feeling tired and exhausted?
- Is your mind clear and able to focus on the needs of the day?
- Do you ever wonder why food is one area of your life you cannot bring under control?
- Do you ever ask, "What is God's standard" in the area of eating?

If you answered yes to any of these questions, you are not alone. Jesus said, *"The thief comes only to steal and kill and destroy; I have come that they may have life, and have it to the full"* (John 10:10). Yet, as we live our lives, many of us seem to be broken down and battling all sorts of physical ailments. God, as our Creator, knows all about the functions of our physical bodies. He did not create us to live in sickness, but in health. God says that if we obey His Word, we will have "life and prosperity" and "blessings," we will "live and increase," it will "go well with them and their children forever," and He will "prolong your days."[1] Jesus came as our Healer—first and foremost as our spiritual healer—but also as our physical healer. Jesus spent much time healing as recorded in the gospels,[2] and He commissioned his disciples to do the same. In Matthew 10:7-8, speaking to his disciples, He said, *"As you go, preach this message: 'The kingdom of heaven is near.' Heal the sick, raise the dead, cleanse those who have leprosy, drive out demons. Freely you have received, freely give."* God loves to see his people healthy, and He loves to heal us!

For the kingdom of God is not a matter of eating and drinking, but of righteousness, peace, and joy in the Holy Spirit.
Romans 14:17

There is sickness in this world. It has been passed down for generations, ever since Adam sinned and death came into the world. But how much sickness and disease are self-induced or made worse by unhealthy lifestyle choices? If God desires to heal us as He shows in His Word, why are we tired, overweight, depressed, and sick?

God has given us a body that runs on fuel, which is healthy food. Do we really know which foods bring health to our bodies? Most people think of carrots and celery sticks, tasteless salads, and bland cooked vegetables. It just doesn't seem practical or appealing to eat this way! Are we correct in our own perception of healthy food? Does it really make a difference if we eat healthy foods, versus the standard American diet? Look around and you will see that obesity is rampant, as are all of the diseases that accompany a diet high in fat and lacking in vital nutrients ... *heart disease, stroke, cancer,* and *diabetes.* Let's not forget the diseases and disorders we might consider less serious, which are nevertheless debilitating for each person who suffers from them, conditions such as: *fibromyalgia, arthritis, chronic fatigue syndrome, digestive disorders, gall stones, kidney stones, clogged arteries, hemorrhoids, high cholesterol, and high blood pressure.* In addition, we have a host of other health issues that are plaguing us, such as *headaches, migraines, allergies, fatigue, sleep disorders, constipation, depression, attention deficit disorder, and skin disorders.* The list goes on and on! Do you experience any of these conditions yourself? What about your friends, family, and neighbors? Are there other ailments you or your loved ones suffer from that are not mentioned above?

We are indeed much more than what we eat, but what we eat can nevertheless help us to be much more than what we are.
Adelle Davis

Here is a very important question that every one of us should ask: *Could these diseases and debilitating conditions be caused or made worse by the foods we eat?* To put it another way, how would our bodies benefit if we transitioned to a truly healthy diet? Let's explore God's Word to gain an understanding of the foods He created that will nourish our bodies, and those that might be harmful.

Chapter 2 Study Questions

1. Answer the following questions:

◆ Do you have physical pain in your body on a regular basis (back ache, joint pain, head ache, etc.)?

◆ Do you sleep well and awaken refreshed, or do you have restless sleep, and awaken tired?

◆ Are you overweight or struggling to maintain your weight?

◆ Do you suffer from depression, high cholesterol, reflux disease, or any other conditions for which you are on prescription medication?

◆ Do you believe you are out of control in the area of eating?

◆ Do you often eat more than you think you should and feel guilty?

◆ Do you often eat foods you know are unhealthy for your body?

◆ Do you go through your day with energy and vigor, or do you drag through the day feeling tired and exhausted?

◆ Is your mind clear and able to focus on the needs of the day?

◆ Do you ever wonder why food is one area of your life you cannot bring under control?

◆ Do you ever ask, "What is God's standard" in the area of eating?

2. Based on your answers, how would you describe the role of food in your life?

   _____

   _____

   _____

3. Describe your current level of health. Use your answers above and the list of health conditions on pages 15-16 as a reference.

   _____

   _____

   _____

4. What did Jesus commission the disciples to do in Matthew 10:7-8?

   _____

   _____

   _____

5. Based on John 10:10, Satan is a _____ who comes to _____, _____, and _____. Why did Jesus come?

   _____

   _____

   _____

6. Are you experiencing victory in the realm of physical health? Explain your answer.

     _____

     _____

     _____

7. Do you believe Jesus wants you to be healthy and victorious in the area of physical health? Explain.

     _____

     _____

     _____

8. List three scriptures illustrating God's desire to heal us.

     _____

     _____

     _____

9. List at least five benefits of walking in abundant health.

     _____

     _____

     _____

     _____

     _____

10. Will you commit to learning about the physical body God made for you and how to properly nourish and care for it? Are you ready to begin achieving abundant health?

_____

_____

_____

11. Write a prayer expressing your heart to the Lord. Ask Him to open your heart to receive His perspective and His wisdom in the area of health and wholeness.

_____

_____

_____

_____

_____

_____

Chapter Three

Following Scripture Like a Recipe

All Scripture is God breathed and is useful for teaching, rebuking, correcting and training in righteousness, so that the man of God may be thoroughly equipped for every good work.
2 Timothy 3:16

We want to be certain when searching God's Word that we do not exclude the valuable wisdom contained in the Old Testament. God gave the Old Testament law for the good of the people and their well-being, in order that He would be glorified. Remember that God created us to bring glory to Himself. God set His standard in the law; therefore, the Israelites knew specifically how to live—what was good or evil, right or wrong, and even the specifics of what constituted food for them. In Malachi 3:6a, God says, *"I the Lord do not change."* Hebrews 13:8 says, *"Jesus Christ is the same yesterday and today and forever."* We can deduce, therefore, that both the Old and New Testaments are valuable to us for whatever information we are seeking regarding all subjects. The Bible is our sourcebook for life.

Because Jesus died on the cross, we are no longer under the law, but under grace. What does this mean? It means that Jesus Christ freed us from the ultimate consequence of sin, which is eternal damnation. He became our sin offering (Romans 8:3), so that we might live. *"For sin shall not be your master, because you are not under law, but under grace"* (Romans 6:14). Remember that God's law exposes sin. *"Therefore no one will be declared righteous in his sight by observing the law; rather, through the law we become conscious of sin"* (Romans 3:20). Should we trample God's grace by continually disregarding the law? Romans 6:15 says, *"What then? Shall we sin because we are not under law but under grace? By no means!"* God's Law is God's Word, which is God. John 1:1 says, *"In the beginning was the Word, and the Word was with God and the Word was God."* Christians growing in spiritual maturity must take all of God's Word into account. We must love all of God's Word!

"Praise the Lord, O my soul; all my inmost being, praise his holy name. Praise the Lord, O my soul, and forget not all his benefits—who forgives all your sins and heals all your diseases, who redeems your life from the pit and crowns you with love and compassion, who satisfies your desires with good things so that your youth is renewed like the eagle's."
Psalm 103:1-5

Let's meditate on the beauty of God's Law as we consider the following passages.

Blessed are they whose ways are blameless, who walk according to the law of the Lord. Blessed are they who keep his statutes and seek him with all their heart. They do nothing wrong; they walk in his ways. You have laid down precepts that are to be fully obeyed. Oh, that my ways were steadfast in obeying your decrees! Then I would not be put to shame when I consider all your commands. I will praise you with an upright heart as I learn your righteous laws. I will obey your decrees; do not utterly forsake me.
Psalm 119: 1-8

How can a young man keep his way pure? By living according to your word. I seek you with all my heart; do not let me stray from your commands. I have hidden your word in my heart that I might not sin against you. Praise be to you, O Lord; teach me your decrees. With my lips I recount all the laws that come from your mouth. I rejoice in following your statutes as one rejoices in great riches. I meditate on your precepts and consider your ways. I delight in your decrees;
I will not neglect your word.
Psalm 119:9-16

⟿⟿

Open my eyes that I may see wonderful things in your law.
Psalm 119:18

⟿⟿

Your statutes are my delight; they are my counselors.
Psalm 119:24

⟿⟿

We love God; therefore, we love His Word from beginning to end. Although we are no longer bound by law, we are free to follow it under grace. The principles of God's Word are truly magnificent and life giving!

God is sovereign. He created us, and He knows us inside and out. If we have questions about our body, soul, or spirit, we should first and foremost go to God's Word and learn His precepts. He delights in our desire to seek Him first, and is pleased when our heart is yearning to know Him through His Word.

...for it is God who works in you to will and to act according to his good purpose.
Philippians 2:13

"Therefore I urge you, brothers, in view of God's mercy, to offer your bodies as living sacrifices, holy and pleasing to God—this is your spiritual act of worship. Do not conform any longer to the pattern of this world, but be transformed by the

23

renewing of your mind. Then you will be able to test and approve what God's will is—his good, pleasing, and perfect will" (Romans 12:1-2). This scripture is revolutionary! We are to *offer* our *bodies* to God. We must not conform but be transformed. Then we will be able to test and approve what God's good, pleasing, and perfect will is. In order to fulfill the mandate in this passage, we must study God's Word and apply it to our lives. We are not our own. Jesus died so that we might live. *"Do you not know that your body is a temple of the Holy Spirit, who is in you, whom you have received from God? You are not your own; you were bought at a price. Therefore honor God with your body"* (1 Corinthians 6:19-20). We should not resemble the world but rather our Creator.

To Eat, or Not to Eat...

Following are some scriptures regarding food that you might have considered inapplicable or obsolete. I propose to you that the standards God gave the Israelites for eating were for their physical benefit, and still apply to us today. It is true that we are not under the law, but rather under grace. We are not talking about salvation, but of accepting God's best. These dietary guidelines may seem a little strange, but if we look at them carefully, we will see that it is for the benefit of our physical bodies that we follow them.

"'This is a lasting ordinance for the generations to come wherever you live: You must not eat any fat or any blood.'"
Leviticus 3:17

The Lord said to Moses, "Say to the Israelites: 'Do not eat any of the fat of cattle, sheep or goats.'"
Leviticus 7:22-23

The Lord said to Moses and Aaron, "Say to the Israelites; 'Of all the animals that live on land, these are the ones you may eat: You may eat any animal that has a split hoof completely divided and that chews the cud. There are some that only chew the cud or only have a split hoof, but you must not eat them.'"
Leviticus 11:1-4a

"These are the animals you may eat: the ox, the sheep, the goat, the deer, the gazelle, the roe deer, the wild goat, the ibex, the antelope and the mountain sheep."
Deuteronomy 14:4-5

"'Of all the creatures living in the water of the seas and streams, you may eat any that have fins and scales. But all creatures in the seas or streams that do not have fins and scales—whether among all the swarming things or among all the other living creatures in the water—you are to detest. And since you are to detest them, you must not eat their meat and you must detest their carcasses. Anything living in the water that does not have fins and scales is to be detestable to you.'"
Leviticus 11:9-12

"'These are the birds you are to detest and not eat because they are detestable: the eagle, the vulture, the black vulture, the red kite, any kind of black kite, any kind of raven, the horned owl, the screech owl, the gull, any kind of hawk, the little owl, the cormorant, the great owl, the white owl, the desert owl, the osprey, the stork, any kind of heron, the hoopoe and the bat.'"
Leviticus 11:13-19

"'All flying insects that walk on all fours are to be detestable to you. There are, however, some winged creatures that walk on all fours that you may eat: those that have jointed legs for hopping on the ground. Of these you may eat any kind of locust, katydid, cricket, or grasshopper. But all other winged creatures that have four legs you are to detest.'"
Leviticus 11:20-23

"'Of all the animals that walk on all fours, those that walk on their paws are unclean for you'"
Leviticus 11:27a

"'Of the animals that move about on the ground, these are unclean for you: the weasel, the rat, any kind of great lizard, the gecko, the monitor lizard, the wall lizard, the skink and the chameleon.'"
Leviticus 11:29-30

"'You must distinguish between the unclean and the clean, between living creatures that may be eaten and those that may not be eaten.'"
Leviticus 11:47

Look closely at the types of animals that God lists as unclean. Do you see a pattern? What trait do the unclean animals share? They are all carnivores or omnivores. That's right. They all feed off of other animal's flesh. The animals God calls clean for us are herbivores—animals that only eat plants.

Look again at the animals of the sea, those that are clean and unclean. The clean fish, including both fins and scales, are fish such as trout, flounder, bass, cod, salmon, grouper, halibut, tuna, mackerel, orange roughy, and perch. These fish and others with fins and scales may be food for us to eat. God tells us that the unclean creatures in the water are to be detestable to us. The King James Version says they are an "abomination" to us. These are very strong words, and much more descriptive than simply being called unclean. Unclean fish include catfish, swordfish, and shark. What are some of these other abominable, detestable creatures? A partial list includes lobster, crab, shrimp, scallops, octopus, oysters, clams, and mussels. These animals are filters of the sea and contain dangerous levels of mercury, cholesterol, chemicals, parasites, bacteria, viruses, and other diseases.

A Scriptural Blueprint

Isn't it interesting that God was so specific in laying out directions pertaining to food, and yet most of us, Christians included, tend to completely disregard them? In searching for health and wholeness in our physical bodies, we first and foremost should study God's Word. What does God say? What is food for us, and what does not constitute food for our physical bodies? There are consequences for disregarding God's statutes. *"Do not be deceived: God cannot be mocked. A man reaps what he sows"* (Galatians 6:7).

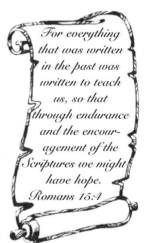

For everything that was written in the past was written to teach us, so that through endurance and the encouragement of the Scriptures we might have hope.
Romans 15:4

Not only do we need to become familiar with the specific list of "do's" and "don'ts" regarding food, but we must also seek out the truth regarding what is truly nourishing and life-giving to our physical bodies. If God did not create us to live in sickness, then He created us to live in health, and He gave us the blueprint for being able to do so! Because God created us, He knows the foods that will perfectly nourish our bodies.

Where did God place Adam and Eve? He put them in a garden—a beautiful, lush garden, with rivers and *"all kinds of trees that were pleasing to the eye and good for food"* (Genesis 2:9a).

He gave them these instructions: *"I give you every seed-bearing plant on the face of the whole earth and every tree that has fruit with seed in it. They will be yours for food"* (Genesis 1:29). God gave Adam and Eve a vegetarian diet, consisting completely of foods grown from the ground. Interestingly enough, He also gave the animals a vegetarian diet. Genesis 1:30 says, *"'And to all the beasts of the earth and all the birds of the air and all the creatures that move on the ground—everything that has the breath of life in it—I give every green plant for food.'"* So it was until the days of Noah.

After the flood God gave further instructions regarding food, which were much more encompassing than the first. God said to Noah, *"'Everything that lives and moves will be food for you. Just as I gave you the green plants, I now give you everything. But you must not eat meat that has its lifeblood in it'"* (Genesis 9:3-4). This passage was God's mandate regarding food until He gave further, clear and concise instructions to the Israelites in the desert, which were described earlier in this chapter. It is interesting to note that although the teaching on clean and unclean animals had not yet been recorded in Scripture, Noah had an understanding of clean and unclean animals, as we see from the sacrifice he offered God after leaving the ark. *"Then Noah built an altar to the Lord and, taking some of all the clean animals and clean birds, he sacrificed burnt offerings on it"* (Genesis 8:20).

> *Truth does not change according to our ability to stomach it.*
> Flannery O'Connor

Let's look back to creation, in Genesis. What foods did God give Adam and Eve in the garden? He gave them *"every seed-bearing plant"* and *"every tree that has fruit with seed in it"* (Genesis 1:29), which included vegetables, fruits, grains, beans, legumes, nuts, seeds, and herbs. They were vegetation eaters, vegetarians, and that is what their bodies were *created* to thrive on. There was no death in the garden, no killing of animals for food, and death from sickness. God created our bodies to be nourished and full of life from vegetables, fruits, grains, beans, legumes, nuts, seeds, and herbs. It wasn't until after the flood that God allowed man to eat animals. God gave very specific guidelines to Moses, Aaron, and the Israelites as to what constituted food, and what animals were not to be considered food.

I will not attempt to answer all of the questions as to why God's dietary guidelines changed for humans at specific points in history. Knowing His will for me in my life, and for the health He desires for me, however, I can use His guidelines of the past as mine today. We were *created* as vegetarians—God *allows* us to eat meat. If we do choose to eat meat, how often are we eating it? Are we following God's guidelines in Leviticus for choosing those animal foods that will bring life and health, not sickness and death? This pattern of thought is not the status quo for today's society, but look at all of the sickness and death in our society today. Why aren't we living healthy lives? Why are the medical and prescription drug industries thriving? Why are Christians just as sick as non-Christians? These are tough questions to answer. We are God's heritage and were created in His image. He does not desire that we live tired and exhausted lives with diseased bodies. *"Beloved, I pray that in all respects you may prosper and be in good health, just as your soul prospers"* (3 John 2, NASB). May you know the freedom God gives to those who obey and walk in His ways!

So be careful to do what the Lord your God has commanded you; do not turn aside to the right or to the left. Walk in all the way that the Lord your God has commanded you, so that you may live and prosper and prolong your days in the land you will possess. Deuteronomy 5:32-33

If some of the scriptures and principles in this chapter have taken you by surprise, I encourage you to return to the scriptures, meditate on them, and ask the Lord to help you understand the principles set forth and how they apply to you. In the next chapter we will begin to explore the beautiful way in which God created our miraculous bodies to live in health, not sickness! Let's pray.

Dear Heavenly Father,

Your Word is truly amazing and life-giving! Thank you for being so specific that You have given us everything we need to know for life and godliness.[1] I confess that I have not been diligent in seeking out your truth in all areas of my life, including the proper care of my physical body. Please forgive me, Lord, for looking at my body from the world's perspective, rather than yours. I pray that you would begin to give me a full understanding of just how miraculous my body actually is, and how to properly care for it the way you designed in order to maintain optimum health. Lord, I want to serve you in full capacity all the days you have set before me. Please give me wisdom in how to live my life in a way that is fully pleasing to you. Thank you for your generous love and grace.

In Jesus' Name,
Amen

Chapter 3 Study Questions

1. What is your perspective regarding Old Testament Law and its value to Christians today?

   _____

   _____

   _____

2. According to Romans 5:18-21, how do we obtain right-eousness?

   _____

   _____

   _____

3. Read Romans 8:1-4, 1 John 3:4, and Romans 7:7. What is the purpose or function of Old Testament Law to the modern day believer?

   _____

   _____

   _____

4. Read and summarize Romans 2:12-13.

   _____

   _____

   _____

5. Write 1 Corinthians 15:10.

    _____

    _____

    _____

6. What enables us to live by the principles of God's Law?

    _____

    _____

    _____

7. According to Romans 12:1, what do we offer as living sacrifices to the Lord?

    _____

    _____

    _____

8. List five practical ways you can offer your body to God:

    _____

    _____

    _____

    _____

    _____

9. List the foods that God gave to Adam and Eve:

_____

_____

_____

10. Briefly describe the dietary laws that God gave to the Israelites.

_____

_____

_____

11. How does your daily diet compare to the foods that God gave to Adam and Eve and those He specified as food for the Israelites?

_____

_____

_____

12. What relationship do you think your diet has on your level of health?

_____

_____

_____

13. In what way has the Word of God spoken to you in this chapter?

   _____

   _____

   _____

14. Have you offered *your* body to the Lord for His service? Have you given Him *all* of you, or only part? Take some time now to offer your whole body to the Lord. He created you to worship Him—body, soul, and spirit. Ask the Lord to show you any areas in the physical realm where you have not given Him full reign. Dedicate yourself to the Lord and begin to trust that His grace, mercy, and strength are sufficient to enable you to fulfill His will in your life.

   _____

   _____

   _____

Chapter Four

Kneading God's Wisdom ... What Fills Your Vessel?

For you created my inmost being; you knit me together in my mother's womb. I praise you because I am fearfully and wonderfully made; your works are wonderful, I know that full well.
Psalm 139:13-14

*T*ake a look at the amazing human being God created when He formed and fashioned you into His image. God created a wonderfully marvelous body! Consider all the intricacies starting from the outside and looking inward. Look at your facial features: your hair, eyes, eyelashes, lips, nose, and ears. Look at your hands and feet, fingers and toes, skin and fingernails. Think of the approximately one hundred trillion living cells God created in you that keep regenerating, minute after minute, day after day, year after year. Each organ in your body has a purpose, and each system works together so that you can function at your highest level. God created an amazing body!

Your body also was created by God to heal itself. Just look at a cut you get on your skin. Immediately after you receive a wound, your body goes to work healing it. What a miracle! Your body was designed to heal itself when it is damaged, however the damage occurred. The inside of your body is no different. Even when you have high blood pressure or high cholesterol, diabetes or cancer, your body wants to rid itself of this condition and recover to a continual state of health. Your body is constantly working and striving to maintain optimum health. Consider what happens when you come in contact with germs from a cold or the flu. Your body immediately fights these invaders, and its degree of success depends on the fuel, or nutrients it contains. Why do some people who come in contact with bacteria and viruses rarely get sick, and when they do the illness is mild and short-lived? Contrast those people with others (and possibly yourself) who seem to catch everything that goes around. Take this as a sign of health or lack of it. If you are frequently sick, your body is engaged in battle, and likely does not have the proper building blocks to effectively fight the intruders. The remedy for this situation is not difficult or complicated. Simply give your body the proper fuel, and it will quickly begin to heal itself.

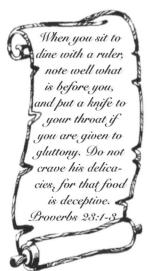

When you sit to dine with a ruler, note well what is before you, and put a knife to your throat if you are given to gluttony. Do not crave his delicacies, for that food is deceptive.
Proverbs 23:1-3

Do you feel so good that sickness is not a concern in your daily life? Are you fearful of disease, believing it is a three headed monster that could creep up at any time, or do you rest assured that God created an amazing body that will constantly be cleansing and rebuilding itself to maintain health? Can you put your focus on the things of God rather than yourself, or are you consumed with pain, excess weight, or disease? Remember, God created you to live in health, not sickness. If you have abused your body by eating processed, devitalized foods, smoking, partaking of other bad habits, or not exercising, you can change these factors and truly begin to nourish your body. Then your body will be able to heal itself naturally, which is what God created it to do.

Do **You** Believe Satan's Lies?

Whether by Satan, our flesh, or both, we have been deceived into believing that sickness and disease are to be normal and natural aspects of our lives. Considering that the first temptation known to man and the first sin involved food, it should be no surprise that to this day Satan still tempts and deceives in this area, and we continue to believe his lies.

"Now the serpent was more crafty than any of the wild animals the Lord God had made. He said to the woman, 'Did God really say, "You must not eat from any tree in the garden?"' The woman said to the serpent, 'We may eat fruit from the trees in the garden, but God did say, "You must not eat fruit from the tree that is in the middle of the garden, and you must not touch it, or you will surely die. 'You will not surely die,' the serpent said to the woman. 'For God knows that when you eat of it, your eyes will be opened, and you will be like God, knowing good and evil.' When the woman saw that the fruit of the tree was good for food and pleasing to the eye, and also desirable for gaining wisdom, she took some and ate it. She also gave some to her husband, who was with her, and he ate it. Then the eyes of both of them were opened, and they realized they were naked; so they sewed fig leaves together and made coverings for themselves."
(Genesis 3:1-7)

The first thing Satan did was to draw Eve's attention to the only forbidden fruit in the entire garden. Eve knew that she could eat freely of any tree in the garden except the tree of knowledge of good and evil. She even verbalized God's instructions, yet when Satan challenged them, she did not refute what he said. Eve considered Satan's words and believed them, even though they conflicted with God's Word. Remember, Satan is crafty and uses a deceptive thought process. Eve listened to him and ate the fruit. Adam also ate, and they suffered immeasurable consequences. Does this scenario sound similar to what is happening today? Satan does not encourage satisfaction with the wonderful foods God has created for us. He is still at the game of deception, and our flesh falls right in line with his tricks and ploys to weaken us beyond measure, even to death.

Envision with me for a moment a world where Christians are healthy, vibrant, and strong. They are physically and emotionally prepared to walk in God's will continuously, and have more than enough energy to fulfill all God has called them to do each

For you make me glad by your deeds, O Lord; I sing for joy at the works of your hands. Psalm 92:4

and every day. Does this sound too good to be true? Satan would have you think it couldn't become true for even one of us, but God's Word says otherwise. Those who are physically healthy tend to be emotionally healthy as well. Our bodies have a way of balancing things out when they have the proper tools to work with. Satan would have us believe there is nothing we can do to prevent disease. He

would have us think that we can't change the way we eat, that it is just too difficult or unimportant. He would have us believe this is just the way life is. And on top of that, he would be delighted if we were living in fear over it all. He doesn't want us to be *"blameless and pure, children of God without fault in a crooked and depraved generation, in which you shine like stars in the universe as you hold out the word of life"* (Philippians 2:15-16a). Satan would do anything in his attempt to stop us from being the *"salt of the earth"* (Matthew 5:13a) or the *"light of the world"* (Matthew 5:14a).

It's time we become wise to Satan's demises and realize that our weak flesh has been falling right in line with his plan. *We are eating foods that are destroying our bodies, and we are suffering the consequences for it.*

There is a better way, and the information is readily available. I will get you started by sharing with you some facts and statistics with the hope that it will spark your interest to further explore all the wonderful ways to care for your body and maintain optimum health. So let's dig in!

Exploring A Better Way

First let's acknowledge that God gave us our bodies to care for, nurture, and maintain health to the best of our abilities, so we can serve Him wholeheartedly. Let us also agree that God has given us all we need for life and godliness, including the knowledge and wisdom of how to care for our physical bodies in order to maintain a healthy state. *"His divine power has given us everything we need for life and godliness through our knowledge of him who called us by his own glory and goodness"* (2 Peter 1:3).

We do not have to be experts in the field of medicine to maintain a healthy body for a lifetime. In fact, being experts in the field of medicine will not help with health and prevention of disease, but only with medical treatment once disease has occurred. Since our goal is to maintain health in the first place, we need information other than what the medical doctors are able to offer. This may be a bold statement, but we need to consider the lack of training in health and nutrition a medical doctor receives. According to George H. Malkmus in *God's Way to Ultimate Health*, only 29 out of 129 accredited medical schools in America require any nutrition classes at all, and of those 29 schools, students of medicine receive less than three hours of training in nutrition. Doctors are trained in diagnosing conditions that already exist, and treating them with drugs and surgery. Most drugs do not cure disease and bring the body to optimum health, but only manage or mask symptoms. Pharmaceutical drugs are foreign substances that your body makes an attempt to remove. They are chemicals that do not belong in your body, and your body reacts to them by causing more sickness in other areas (side effects).

The Lord is my light and my salvation—whom shall I fear? The Lord is the stronghold of my life—of whom shall I be afraid? Psalm 27:1

Our approach to health and wellness is focused in the wrong area. The best path is that of unending good health—preventing disease from taking root in the first place, and healing naturally when possible through proper care of the body. Doctors are not the *source* of health and wellness. Their primary focus is diagnosing and treating with medication. They do not heal. God heals, and He created your own body to heal itself. God can and does heal miraculously, but we must take responsibility for the proper care of this temple in order to be good stewards of what the Lord has given us. We have strayed so far from the healthy road, it is imperative that we find our way back. Then we can experience the magnificent benefits of having a truly healthy body.

Romans 12: 1-2 says, *"Therefore, I urge you, brothers, in view of God's mercy, to offer your bodies as living sacrifices, holy and pleasing to God—this is your spiritual act of worship. Do not conform any longer to the pattern of this world, but be transformed by the renewing of your mind. Then you will be able to test and approve what God's will is—his good, pleasing, and perfect will."* Your spiritual act of worship is to offer your body as a living sacrifice, holy and pleasing to God. Notice this scripture does not say "offer your spirits" or "offer your souls," but *"offer your bodies."* Dwell on this for a moment—offer your body as a living sacrifice. A sacrifice could not crawl off the altar and do as it wished. Its master gave it up for an even greater good: to please God. A sacrifice does nothing of its own accord, only what pleases the master. *"Do not conform any longer to the pattern of this world"* denotes that we already have conformed to the pattern of this world, and we are to stop and renew our mind with God's Word. Then we will know what His good, pleasing, and perfect will is for us. How many of us ignore God's good, pleasing, and perfect will because we choose to ignore how God designed our physical bodies? How many of us cook more for taste than nutrition? How many know from God's Word and those who have studied His masterpiece, the human body,

The secret of success is constancy to purpose.
Benjamin Disraeli

how to properly nourish and care for it? Proper care of our physical bodies is something we must learn and practice.

"Do not merely listen to the word, and so deceive yourselves. Do what it says. Anyone who listens to the word but does not do what it says is like a man who looks at his face in a mirror and, after looking at himself, goes away and immediately forgets what he looks like. But the man who looks intently into the perfect law that gives freedom, and continues to do this, not forgetting what he has heard, but doing it—he will be blessed in what he does" (James 1:22-25). Did you hear that? God's perfect law gives freedom! But it comes at the cost of searching intently, studying, and applying God's truth, and not forgetting what we have heard. Is this a high cost for the blessings of the Lord? I don't think so. He gave himself up on the cross for us. I think I can give up my favorite (body abusing) junk foods in exchange for God's blessings and promises. As a matter of fact, the extent to which we sacrifice our own fleshly desires is the extent to which we receive God's blessings in our physical bodies. If we sow good seed (proper care of our bodies) we will reap a good harvest (health).

Soda in Your Gas Tank ... Candy for Your Cat?

Many people have told me that they just don't believe that what they eat causes their physical ailments, or really has anything to do with the overall functioning of their body; however, we have to face the facts. There are certain universal truths that we cannot deny. If you don't believe in gravity, I still wouldn't suggest you jump off your roof, because evidence has shown you will fall to the ground. The law of gravity is in action, whether or not you believe in it, as are all of God's universal laws.

Have you ever seen a person who feeds his dog in the same manner that he himself eats? More often than not, the dog owner says, "Don't let him eat that, it will make him sick" or "It will make him fat," or "He won't be healthy if he eats table food." So a dog is worse off when he eats a hamburger on a white bun, or

French fries, or a sugary dessert? What about your body? How does it fare on these substances? Is it truly healthy?

God created our bodies to run efficiently on a wide variety of foods, but there are many substances you will find in your local grocery store today that are not on that list. Would you pour soda in your gas tank? Would you wash your hair with Crisco? Would you feed your cat a candy bar and a sugary drink several days a week? Sounds a little crazy, but we do much crazier things by ingesting these substances ourselves! If you think Crisco (hydrogenated oil) would be difficult to get out of your hair, how about your blood vessels?

I implore you to take responsibility for the foods you put into your body. Ask the Lord if the foods you eat are good and pleasing to Him. Educate yourself on which foods are truly nourishing and which are detrimental to your health. Start by believing that the God who created you wants what is best for you, and has provided a roadmap for you to follow. Believe that He does give you an alternative to sickness and degenerative disease, if only you choose His way, not your own! Then have faith that God will hold you up during your time of learning, that He will forgive your past mistakes and redeem your physical body for His glory, regardless of what state it is currently in. He made you and He so lovingly cares for you in every aspect of your life. Will you follow His plan for your physical body as well as your spirit?

"Therefore, since we are surrounded by such a great cloud of witnesses, let us throw off everything that hinders and the sin that so easily entangles, and let us run with perseverance the race marked out for us. Let us fix our eyes on Jesus, the author and perfecter of our faith, who for the joy set before him endured the cross, scorning it's shame, and sat down at the right hand of the throne of God. Consider him who endured such opposition from sinful men, so that you will not grow weary and lose heart."
Hebrews 12:1-3

Chapter 4 Study Questions

1. Up until this point, what has been your belief pertaining to sickness, disease, and healing?

    _____

    _____

    _____

2. List any health conditions you or your loved ones suffer from.

    _____

    _____

    _____

3. Are you fearful of any diseases in particular? If so, which ones?

    _____

    _____

    _____

4. Find and write two Scriptures where the Lord tells us not to fear.

    _____

    _____

    _____

5. In what ways do you believe Satan is deceiving us through food?

_____

_____

_____

6. Write Romans 12:1-2.

_____

_____

_____

How have you conformed to the pattern of this world regarding food?

_____

_____

_____

7. Write the definition of steward.

_____

_____

_____

List three ways you can be a good steward of your physical body.

_____

_____

_____

8. Read Matthew 19:16-22. What correlation can you make between the rich young man and riches, and people and food?

_____

_____

_____

9. Has the Lord ever spoken to you regarding your eating habits? _____

   What was your response?

_____

_____

_____

10. Write two Scriptures regarding freedom.

_____

_____

_____

11. According to Philippians 2:13, it is _____ who works in you to will and to act according to his good purpose.

12. Do you desire better health? _____

    Would you like to have more energy, increased stamina, a clear mind, and no fear of disease? _____

    Do you believe that with proper care of your body, you can become healthy and vibrant? _____

    Will you take responsibility for your health and well-being by learning to properly care for and abundantly nourish your body? _____

～#～

If you answered yes to these questions, it's time to quit playing defense and begin playing offense. Go on the offensive against sickness and disease. Give your body the tools it needs to fight these invaders before they arrive.

Are you ready to take this challenge? Then take some time now to dedicate your body to God. Choose to be a good steward of the only body He gave you for this life on earth. Recognize its value and determine to keep it in tip-top shape so you can serve your creator in full capacity all the days of your life. Express your desire to God to maintain a healthy body for His service and for His glory. Ask for God's wisdom and strength, and for His will to be done in your life. If you are a willing vessel, God will move in your life and on your behalf. To God be the glory!

Chapter Five

Pleasing Your Palate
With Scriptures' Simple Menu

Take wheat and barley, beans and lentils, millet and spelt; put them in a storage jar and use them to make bread for yourself.
Ezekiel 4:9a

Many people believe that eating healthy is an ambiguous term, and some believe it is a relative term. Still others believe that it requires strong will-power, hunger pangs, lots of money, and self sacrifice. I am here to tell you that both God and scientists have defined the same healthy eating standards. When we take a look at the foods God gave Adam and Eve, the foods the Israelites and others in the Old Testament ate, and the foods those in the New Testament ate, including Jesus, we see that eating the foods God designed for our bodies to thrive on is neither difficult nor complicated. God created in us a natural hunger for good foods, but it is masked because of our habits from childhood and from giving in to our fleshly cravings. Refined foods are addictive. If we eat them on a regular basis, our bodies will crave them. We find ourselves eating foods in an attempt to satisfy our fleshly cravings rather than responding to our God given desire for good, wholesome food.

What foods has God designed for us to eat? First let's go back to Genesis, where God gave Adam and Eve *"every seed-bearing plant on the face of the whole earth and every tree that has fruit with seed in it"* (Genesis 1:29). These foods include vegetables, fruits, grains, beans, legumes, nuts, seeds, and herbs. Adam and Eve ate their foods unrefined, and many believe they also were not cooked.

God created our bodies to live and thrive on plant foods. Scripture confirms that man thrived on plant foods for hundreds of years. God created our bodies to be completely healthy when eating plant foods, with no need for meat. Remember that God gave new instructions to Noah, and again to the Israelites. The Israelites then had clear parameters for eating meat as well as vegetables. Even though the Israelites *could* eat meat, they apparently did not eat it on a regular basis. Only people of great wealth had enough animals that they could slaughter one for a meal. The majority of people living at that time lived on grains, grain bread, vegetables, fruits, and beans.[1] Those living by the sea ate more fish, which when taken from clean waters can be a beneficial food. The main sustenance of people all through time has been vegetables, fruits, grains, beans, legumes, nuts, seeds, and herbs. These foods have been proven by science to enhance a long, healthy, productive life. So we see that eating healthy is not complicated! We have complicated it by our desire for rich foods that have been tampered with, foods that have been refined by adding sugar, preservatives, hydrogenated oil, and other dangerous substances.

Therefore I tell you, do not worry about your life, what you will eat or drink; or about your body, what you will wear. Is not life more important than food, and the body more important than clothes? Matthew 6:25

Take a look at what Daniel chose to eat when faced with the king's foods: *"The king assigned them a daily amount of food and wine from the king's table. They were to be trained for three years, and after that they were to enter the king's service...But Daniel resolved not to defile himself with the royal food and wine, and he asked the chief official for permission not to defile himself this way. Now God had caused the official to show favor and sympathy to Daniel, but the official told Daniel, 'I am afraid of my lord the king, who has assigned your food and drink. Why should he see you looking worse than the other young men your age?'… Daniel then said to the guard … 'Please test your servants for ten days: Give us nothing but vegetables to eat and water to drink. Then compare our appearance with that of the young men who eat the royal food, and treat your servants in accordance with what you see.' So he agreed to this and tested them for ten days. At the end of ten days they looked healthier and better nourished than any of the young men who ate the royal food.*

So the guard took away their choice food and the wine they were to drink and gave them vegetables instead" (Daniel 1:5-16).

Truly amazing! Daniel set aside any fleshly desire for royal food and wine, and chose wisdom instead. The king's foods were known to be rich, fat laden foods. Certain diseases similar to those today were associated with kings. Of course only the wealthy of the land could eat these rich foods, so these diseases seemed to primarily strike the kings.[2] Daniel chose those foods less tampered with, foods served closely to the way God created them. Daniel and his friends were blessed in many ways. *"At the end of the time set by the king to bring them in, the chief official presented them to Nebuchadnezzar. The king talked with them and he found none equal to Daniel, Hananiah, Mishael and Azariah; so they entered the king's service. In every matter of wisdom and understanding about which the king questioned them, he found them ten times better than all the magicians and enchanters in his whole kingdom"* (Daniel 1:18-20).

There's No Doubt About It

Good nutrition is not complex. Eating a variety of whole grains, vegetables, fruits, grains, beans, legumes, nuts, seeds, and herbs gives your body ample nutrition in order to grow properly and avoid disease. The problem is that we don't eat nearly enough of these foods to reap the benefits. What we do eat is an abundance of foods that are literally killing us. Americans as a whole have been deceived into believing that some foods we have eaten our entire lives are not only beneficial but necessary, when in fact the opposite is true. Some information I will be sharing with you may challenge your current understanding of nutrition, but I pray you will set aside your earthly wisdom, and ask God to give you full understanding and revelation as to how to properly nourish your physical body. I also pray that you will continue investigating the topic of food-induced disease, and make necessary dietary changes so you may live an abundant, healthy, and disease-free life.

Thousands of studies have been conducted regarding specific foods and the effects they have on our bodies. Evidence is conclusive as to which foods promote health, and which are detrimental to our lives. We hear so many conflicting reports in the media concerning good health, however, it is no wonder people so readily give up on finding the path to good health. Some of these reports may be true, and some may be false. They are often isolated studies, and we have no way of knowing how scientifically accurate or inaccurate they may be. What I will be addressing are the conclusive findings from thousands of studies that have been read and reviewed by medical doctors and other professionals, who have in turn written entire books based on these findings.

A generous man will himself be blessed, for he shares his food with the poor.
Proverbs 22:9

As much as some people want to believe that we are neither physically responsible nor able to prevent or cure major diseases such as heart disease, cancer, diabetes, and strokes, through a healthy lifestyle, the *fact* is we can. This is wonderful news! The studies are available, and there are many doctors successfully treating their patients in disease reversal through proper nutrition.

Herein lies the big question. If we know which foods are good for us—vegetables, fruits, grains, beans, legumes, nuts, seeds, and herbs—then which foods are killing us? We certainly are eating plenty of them, since the estimate of food induced death of Americans is over 90%.[3] Did you hear that? Over 90% of deaths in America are directly caused by the foods we eat. That means 9 out of every 10 deaths, or more, could be prevented. What a startling statistic!

Consider those suffering from disease. Is not the suffering and pain it causes almost as devastating as the death toll? The *truth* is, most diseases can be prevented, reversed and cured by following the proper dietary guidelines. The sad part of it all is that much to our detriment, we as Christians have bought into the world's propaganda promoting its inferior "food" products, instead of following God's guidelines and eating the foods He created for us. We have not researched good nutrition for ourselves to seek out and find the truth. We just assumed there was no conclusive evidence in the area of food and nutrition. Even worse than that, many of us (most of us!) do not follow the small amount we know to be true. Christians are just as sick as the rest of the world. Does God want this to be so? We have been ignorant in some cases and stubborn in others. Have we allowed food to become an idol in our lives, putting it even before the proper care of our body (temple)?

Never, never, never quit.
Winston Churchill

Exodus 20:4-6 says, *"You shall not make for yourself an idol in the form of anything in heaven above or on the earth beneath or in the waters below. You shall not bow down to them or worship them; for I, the Lord your God, am a jealous God, punishing the children for the sin of the fathers to third and fourth generation of those who hate me, but showing love to a thousand generations of those who love me and keep my commandments."*

Are we bowing down to food? Are we controlled by our fleshly cravings like the Israelites in the desert, who grumbled and complained against the Lord that they could not have the foods they liked and desired? God had provided perfect food for them, but they were not satisfied! God sent the meat the Israelites were "wailing" for, but not out of His good pleasure.

Numbers 11:33-34 says, *"But while the meat was still between their teeth and before it could be consumed, the anger of the Lord burned against the people, and he struck them with a severe plague.*

Therefore the place was named Kibrith Hattaavah, because they buried the people who had craved other food."

Are we satisfied with the food God has given us, or do we choose what best satisfies our fleshly cravings? This question is challenging for all of us, and must be addressed. In all areas of our Christian life, we must look inside and see if we are walking with God or if we are ignoring any part of His Word. He loves us so much that He wants no less than all of us. Somehow the issue of food gets ignored, laughed at, joked about, and casually blown off. Our craving for food and the choices we make are

I wait for the Lord, my soul waits, and in his word I put my hope.
Psalm 130:5

hindering our ability to serve our Lord. Our minds and finances are consumed with food, and many of us are sick and dying. May the God of all grace forgive us, help us to know the truth, and follow it to the fullest.

In the next two chapters we will take a look at the common foods that are harming our bodies rather than strengthening them. This information may differ from what you learned as a child and the eating habits you have carried throughout your adult life. It also differs from what the diet industry is telling us. Don't worry or fret! God created us to live in freedom, and when we learn how to satisfy our body's needs in the area of nutrition, we find great freedom in health and in the wonderful variety of foods God created.

Chapter 5 Study Questions

1. Which foods have been proven to maintain a healthy body?

   _____

   _____

   _____

2. What did Daniel request to eat and drink when he was assigned food from the king's table?

   _____

   _____

3. After the allotted time period, how did Daniel, Hananiah, Mishael, and Azariah compare to the others in the kingdom?

   _____

   _____

   _____

4. Christians are just as sick as non-Christians. Why?

   _____

   _____

   _____

5. Describe the proper place of food in a Christian's life.

   _____

   _____

   _____

   When does food become an idol?

   _____

   _____

   _____

6. In Numbers 11:33-34, why did God become angry with the Israelites?

   _____

   _____

   What was their consequence?

   _____

   _____

7. Describe your relationship with food and the victory or struggles you experience.

   _____

   _____

   _____

8. What specific healthy and life-giving foods are you putting into your body?

_____

_____

_____

9. What foods are you putting into your body that are potentially damaging?

_____

_____

_____

10. We are now ready to study the truth regarding many of the foods we eat on a regular basis. Let's pray together.

Dear Heavenly Father,

I love you and want to serve you with all of my heart and all of my strength. Thank you for creating such an amazing body. Will you forgive me, Lord, for not caring for my body in the proper manner to maintain health and wellness? Please forgive me for craving foods that are not your best for me. I realize now that they have brought sickness and disease, not wellness. Please heal me, and give me wisdom, understanding, and the will to do what is right. May the joy of the Lord be my strength!

In Jesus' Name,

Amen

For I know the plans I have for you, declares the Lord, plans to prosper you and not to harm you, plans to give you hope and a future.
Jeremiah 29:11

Chapter Six

Taking the Lid Off—Exposing the Meat and Dairy Myth

Then you will know the truth, and the truth will set you free.
John 8:32

*T*he information in this chapter may surprise you and even challenge what you think you know about food. I encourage you to be diligent in reading all of the information, and decide how it applies to you. Read on to discover the main culprits of sickness and disease, and how they affect your body.

Meat

There are many causes of illness and death from food, but eating meat undoubtedly ranks number one on the list. Meat is full of fat, cholesterol, and protein. Even lean cuts contain high amounts of cholesterol, because cholesterol is found in the lean tissue. The average American who consumes meat eats over fifty pounds of fat each year![1] Meat and other animal products are responsible for the majority of diseases in our country, including, but not limited to, *cancer, heart disease, diabetes, strokes, gout, skin conditions, hemorrhoids, constipation, kidney dis-*

ease, osteoporosis, obesity, gallstones, arthritis, and diverticulo-sis.[2] If I didn't mention your condition, you might as well place it on the list, because practically all diseases, disorders, and mal-functions of the body can be helped and or corrected when meat and other animal products are removed from our diets.

An estimated 50% of all Americans will die of heart disease.[3] 38% of all Americans will die of cancer,[4] and over 6% of all Americans will suffer from diabetes.[5] These diseases are prima-rily caused by eating animal products and are preventable through proper diet and nutrition. Let us take this information seriously and stop killing ourselves!

The average American's risk of dying from a heart attack is approximately 50%.[6] The average American vegetarian has less than a 4% chance of having a heart attack.[7] Bear in mind that the only source of LDL (bad) cholesterol is in animal products.[8] No person's arteries have ever become clogged from eating too much spinach, barley, or beans (unless, of course, they were cov-ered in animal fat).

One study that particularly stands out among the rest is the China-Cornell-Oxford Project, or the China Project. The study followed people who live in different geographic regions of China, because they usually remain in the general area they were born, and each area has its own dietary traditions. For example, the people of one locale ate a vegetarian diet, while others ate a small amount of animal products, and still others ate animal products on a regular basis. Because the people remained in the same geographic location, they had maintained these dietary practices their entire lives. The results are astounding, and differ greatly from what we have been taught in the past regarding proper nutrition. Here are some highlights of the results of the China Project and other studies:

◆ The consumption of animal products and cancer are interrelated.
◆ Disease is not only caused by animal fat, but by ani-mal protein.

◆ The incidence of cancer is directly proportional to the amount of animal products a person consumes. The more meat a person eats, the more likely he is to develop cancer; conversely, the less meat a person eats, the less likely he is to develop cancer.

◆ Eating legumes two times a week can lower a person's risk of colon cancer by 50%.

◆ The risk of developing breast cancer is 70% higher in those eating meat four times a week, versus those eating meat once a week.

◆ Those populations who consume less than 10% of their calories from fat have virtually no incidences of breast cancer.

◆ There is a correlation between heart disease and animal protein, not just animal fat. Even low fat dairy and chicken raise cholesterol. This means that those who switch from red meat to chicken and fish do not regularly see significant changes in their level of cholesterol or heart disease.

◆ Animal protein raises cholesterol. Plant protein lowers cholesterol.

◆ The people of poor countries who consume very few animal products have less than a 5% incidence of heart attacks.

◆ There is virtually no heart disease and no heart attacks in the populations who are lifelong vegetarians.

◆ Those in China with low rates of disease ate an abundance of fresh vegetables and grains.

◆ The amount of disease protection correlates directly with the number of years a person has remained on a vegetarian diet.

There are some other interesting findings from the China project. Those eating the fewest animal products obtained only 6%

of their calories from fat, and those eating the highest percentage of animal products consumed 24% from fat. Compare this with the average American who consumes 40% of their calories from fat! The American Heart Association suggests that patients lower their overall intake to 30% of fat derived calories, but

So do not fear, for I am with you; do not be dismayed, for I am your God. I will strengthen you and help you; I will uphold you with my righteous right hand. Isaiah 41:10

based on the findings of these and other studies, a 30% intake of fat from calories still promotes disease. This means that not only will the disease currently in your body worsen, but new disease is likely to develop.

Next, the diets of everyone in the study were low in refined foods, so whether they ate meat once a week or more often, they still consumed an abundance of fresh vegetables and whole grains. They did not achieve optimum health by eating low-fat refined and processed foods, such as diet cookies, chips, and beverages. Now we can understand why in one large study, the Nurses Study, those who reduced their fat intake did not have a lower incidence of breast cancer. Although the nurses in this study consumed a "lower-fat" diet, they continued to eat low-fat meat and low-fat refined products, and did not have the benefits of a diet rich in fresh produce. In addition, their version of low-fat was still higher than the highest fat consuming group in the China Project.

As the China Project findings show, the combined benefits from a diet consisting of very few animal products with abundant consumption of unrefined plant foods offer the greatest health benefits.[9]

Early Maturity Linked to Animal Products?

Heart disease and cancer are not the only concerns related to the consumption of meat and other animal products. You may have noticed that children seem to be maturing early these days, and they are. As diets have changed to include more meat, dairy, and refined products, the age of menstruation has continued to decline. The average age of the onset of puberty in 1840 was seventeen according to the World Health Organization, as compared to twelve in American girls today. Not only does early maturity cause problems in society, it is also a risk factor for breast cancer, prostate cancer, and testicular cancer. The earlier a person matures, the greater the risk of these cancers.

Studies show that girls on vegetarian diets who eat a significant amount of complex carbohydrates have a later age of onset of puberty, as well as significantly less acne. Eating animal products increases the amount of hormones in a person's body, leading to early maturation.[10] We have a tendency to think that children are invincible and can handle or even benefit from more meat, cheese, and eggs, but we are setting the stage for disease when we feed our children an abundance of animal products.

Dairy, America's Favorite Fat

The one fat that American's love the most is cheese. Consumption of cheese in America has increased 193% in the last twenty-five years,[11] with devastating results. The average American consumes over 550 pounds of dairy products each and every year![12] Just as with meat, we have been led to believe that dairy, including milk and cheese, is a healthy and beneficial food. But is it? Are milk and other dairy products necessary for optimum health? The truth is, no. Dairy is not beneficial, but is actually harmful to your body, causing many of the same diseases as meat consumption. Dairy is linked to *tendonitis, ischemic heart disease, ovarian cancer, testicular cancer, other cancers, osteoporosis, lymphatic leukemia, multiple sclerosis, kidney stones, Hodgkins disease, gallstones, Crohn's disease, ulcerative colitis, diarrhea, bloating, cramping, asthma, diabetes, congestion, allergies, constipation, eczema, psoriasis, and many other conditions.*[13]

The important thing is this: To be able at any moment to sacrifice what we are for what we could become. Charles Dubois

Cow's milk is intended for baby cows. God designed cow's milk to grow a calf from 45 pounds to 400 pounds in a year. I don't know about you, but I don't want that effect of milk in my body! Cow's milk is made up of 15% protein, while human breast milk is 5% protein. Calves double their weight in 47 days (and have four stomachs, by the way). Humans double their weight much more slowly, in about 180 days. God created human milk to perfectly feed young humans, and cow's milk to perfectly feed young cows. We cause problems for ourselves when we ingest a food that is not designed for our bodies.

Pasteurization and homogenization cause even more problems with assimilation of nutrients and digestion of dairy products. During the pasteurization process, the milk is heated to high temperatures, largely killing the nutrients that could be beneficial, and changing them from an organic to an inorganic state. Homogenization adds yet more complications to the digestion of milk. When milk is homogenized, the fat particles are broken up and put into suspension, allowing substances into our bloodstream that would have otherwise been sifted out. In fresh cow's milk, the cream rises to the top, and in store bought milk, it is all mixed up and cannot be separated. Homogenization causes our body great difficulty in digestion.

In nature, animals do not naturally drink the milk of another animal, they do not consume milk after they are weaned, and their milk is always raw, not pasteurized or homogenized. We have tampered with nature, and are reaping the consequences through sickness and disease.

Dairy and Osteoporosis—You May Be Surprised

After all we hear about the need for more calcium and the risk of bone loss, particularly for women, you might be wondering what the best source of calcium is. We are encouraged by doctors, TV ads, magazine articles, etc. to drink more milk and take calcium supplements. But is their information accurate and scientifically sound? Not according to studies, including some conducted by the National Dairy Council itself.

Americans consume more calcium from dairy and other sources than most people in the world, yet we have one of the highest rates of osteoporosis in the world. How can this be if we are following the advice of the experts, who tell us to drink milk, eat yogurt and cheese, and feed them to our children? How could we possibly still be suffering from bone loss? Studies have shown that the countries that consume the most animal products—America, Finland, and Sweden, for example, have the highest rates of osteoporosis. The countries that consume few animal products, such as China, New Guinea, and the natives of South Africa have the lowest rates of osteoporosis. In fact, where it is a major health crisis in some cultures, it is virtually non-existent in others.[14]

So what causes osteoporosis if it is not lack of calcium in the diet? We have been taught that we need to eat dairy products and take calcium supplements to avoid osteoporosis, but that has not worked! Why not? Because osteoporosis is caused by *loss* of calcium, which occurs when we eat protein from animal sources. Eating animal protein causes your body's fluids and tissues to become acidic, and your body quickly tries to neutralize them by releasing calcium from your bones. The more protein you eat from animal sources, the more calcium loss you will incur. According to studies, those drinking milk have a greater incidence of osteoporosis than those who do not consume dairy products.

Finally, be strong in the Lord and in his mighty power. Put on the full armor of God so that you can take your stand against the devil's schemes.
Ephesians 6:10-11

In Harvard University's *Nurses Health Study,* where 78,000 women were followed over a twelve-year period, researchers found that women who consumed the most calcium from dairy products had the highest incidence of bone fracture.[15] Many other studies cite similar findings. A study funded by the National Dairy Council showed that postmenopausal women who consumed three glasses of milk per day (consuming 1,400 mg of calcium per day from milk) lost bone mass at twice the rate of those who did not consume the milk.[16] Eskimos consume over 2000 mg of calcium a day from soft fish bones, but have a higher rate of hip fracture than any other country in the world.[17] Some other factors that negatively affect bone health are intake of sodium, saturated fat, sugar, caffeine, alcohol, tobacco, steroids, and use of other drugs.

Fruits, vegetables, grains, beans, legumes, nuts and seeds are

They willfully put God to the test by demanding the food they craved.
Psalm 78:18

very beneficial in supplying your body with adequate calcium and preventing bone loss. Studies show that fruits and vegetables are actually protective against bone loss.[18] Plant based foods are the healthiest source of calcium for your body, because they are easily digested without the negative side effects and bone loss resulting from ingesting animal protein. Some beneficial foods that are rich in calcium include, but are not limited to, kale, Swiss chard, turnip greens, mustard greens, dandelion greens, beet greens, cabbage, Chinese cabbage, spinach, broccoli, almonds, figs, sesame seeds, okra, and blackstrap molasses.

Eating these foods as well as a variety of other vegetables, fruits, grains, beans, nuts, and seeds, and limiting the amount of animal products you consume is one of the best ways to maintain bone health. Other beneficial factors include getting enough vitamin D through sun exposure and exercising on a regular basis.

Fish

Calorie for calorie and pound for pound, fish is a better choice of food than other animal products. Jesus ate clean fish (Luke 24:42-43, John 21:9-12) that was fresh, not frozen or canned. On the whole, fish contains far fewer calories and fat per pound than beef, lamb, turkey, ham, and other meats, while providing essential omega-3 fatty acids.

Although eating fresh fish can offer some health benefits, consuming it on a regular basis can cause more harm than good. Fish is one of the most perishable and toxic foods that we consume today. When fish begins to spoil, it produces a fishy odor, which is evidence of harmful bacteria. Chemicals and other pollutants, such as PCBs, mercury, and lead are common in our lakes, rivers, and oceans. These pollutants are concentrated in the flesh, which is what you consume when eating fish. Pollutants in fish have been found to cause a host of health issues, including cancer, brain damage, seizures, birth defects, mental retardation, low immune function, and others.[19]

Choosing clean fish from clean waters makes fish a better choice than other animal products. Limiting your intake of fish while increasing intake of plant foods will help your body achieve its maximum state of health.

Protein

Protein is perhaps one of the most misunderstood requirements of the human body. From faulty studies to misinformation from the meat and dairy industries, we have been indoctrinated with incorrect information, and strongly encouraged to rely on it for the sake of our health. Traditions are difficult to change when the logic for those traditions was established as a child, no matter how faulty the logic may be.

For many years we have been taught that the only good source of protein, and all eight essential amino acids, was from animal products. This information has been proven to be incorrect! Fifteen percent of the human body is made up of protein, ranking second only to water, which comprises 70 percent of the human body. Protein consists of chains of amino acids. There are 23 amino acids, 15 of which your body produces itself. The other eight, called essential amino acids, must be obtained from outside sources.

You, my brothers, were called to be free. But do not use your freedom to indulge the sinful nature; rather, serve one another in love.
Galatians 5:13

Remember, Adam and Eve were created vegetarians, and people lived long fruitful lives on only plant foods for hundreds of years. Plants contain all eight essential amino acids that our bodies don't produce, and they do not have to be combined in any specific way for our body to utilize them. God did not make eating healthy foods and supplying our bodies with proper nutrition difficult! In fact, eating any variety of vegetables, fruits, beans, and whole grains will give you more than enough protein without any help from eating animal products. Have you ever wondered how a gorilla, buffalo, giraffe, or elephant becomes so large while eating only plants? They do not require animal protein to build a strong body, and neither do we!

In today's society where there is so much disease, we have much more reason to be concerned about over-consumption of protein and other potentially harmful substances than we do to be concerned about lack of vital nutrients from a vegetarian diet. Protein is a necessary building block for everyone; conversely, we now have a host of diseases caused by eating too much protein. Some health conditions linked to excess protein consumption are *breast cancer, colon cancer, pancreatic cancer, prostate cancer, other cancers, osteoporosis, arthritis, obesity, high cholesterol, kidney disorders, liver disorders, high blood pressure, bad breath, acid reflux, and shorter life span.*

Recommended daily protein amounts have changed over the years to reflect varying research results. U.S. government recommendations have decreased from 118 grams of protein per day to their current recommendation of 45-55 grams per day.[20] The World Health Organization (WHO) recommends obtaining five percent of daily calories from protein[21] (a minimum of 32 grams for a 150-pound male), and the recommended range from other various organizations is from 2.5 to 8 percent.[22]

How easy is it to get enough protein to maintain optimum health from a vegetarian diet? Very easy, assuming we eat a diet adequate in calories. Figure 6.1 shows the percentage of calories from protein in some common foods:[23]

Beans		Vegetables	
Lentils	29%	Spinach	49%
Split peas	28%	Kale	45%
Kidney beans	26%	Broccoli	45%
Navy beans	26%	Collards	43%
Lima beans	26%	Cauliflower	40%
Chick peas	23%	Parsley	34%
		Lettuce	34%
Grains		Green peas	30%
		Zucchini	28%
Rye	20%	Cucumbers	24%
Wheat	17%	Green pepper	22%
Wild rice	16%	Cabbage	22%
Buckwheat	15%	Celery	21%
Oatmeal	15%	Eggplant	21%
Millet	12%	Tomatoes	18%
Barley	11%	Onions	16%
Brown rice	8%	Beets	15%
		Potatoes	11%
		Sweet Potatoes	6%
Fruits		**Nuts and Seeds**	
Lemons	16%	Pumpkin Seeds	21%
Honeydew		Peanuts	18%
melon	10%	Sunflower Seeds	17%
Cantaloupe	9%	Walnuts	13%
Strawberry	8%	Sesame Seeds	13%
Orange	8%	Almonds	12%
Cherry	8%	Cashews	12%
Grape	8%	Filberts	8%
Watermelon	8%		
Tangerine	7%		
Peach	6%		
Pear	5%		
Banana	5%		
Grapefruit	5%		
Pineapple	3%		
Apple	1%		

Figure 6.1. Calories from protein

Remember that our daily requirement is only approximately 5% of calories from protein, assuming we consume an adequate number of calories.[24] Take another look at the food chart. Most common plant foods, especially beans and vegetables, greatly exceed that level. Eating plenty of vegetables, fruits, grains, beans, legumes, nuts, and seeds that God gave us will supply us with an abundance of the protein and other nutrients our bodies need. For an example of a vegetarian menu that includes more than adequate protein for one day, see page 172.

Other Causes of Concern

Hormones

There is great concern over the amount of hormones, antibiotics and pesticides given to animals, and their effects on humans who consume meat, dairy products, and eggs. Although the U.S. banned the use of DDT in America, it still imports foods containing DDT.[25] You may be surprised to learn that the greatest concentration of dangerous chlorinated hydrocarbon pesticides, such as dioxin and DDT, is in meat. John Robbins estimates that these dangerous chemicals in our foods are in the following proportions: 55% from meat, 23% from dairy products, 6% from vegetables, 4% from fruits, and 1% from grains.[26] The EPA found that over 99% of mothers' milk sampled in the U.S. contained significant levels of DDT and PCB's, yet breast milk from American vegetarians contained only 1-2% of the levels of these harmful chemicals as the national average.[27]

Bovine Growth Hormone, which is banned in most countries, is commonly used in America's dairy cows to increase their milk production with devastating results, including mastitis in the cows. Milk from cows given BGH can contain pus resulting from the frequent cases of mastitis, as

It takes a lot of courage to release the familiar and seemingly secure, to embrace the new. But there is no real security in what is no longer meaningful. There is more security in the adventurous and exciting, for in movement there is life, and in change there is power. Alan Cohen

well as antibiotics that were used to treat mastitis. And who wants to be drinking hormones, anyway?

Antibiotics

We have all heard about different strains of bacteria becoming resistant to antibiotics, and many believe it is simply from overuse of antibiotics by humans. Did you know that an estimated 55% of all antibiotics used in the United States are fed to livestock on a routine basis to promote growth, improve reproduction, prevent disease, and treat disease? According to John Robbins, 90% of staphylococci bacteria are resistant to penicillin, compared to less than 10% in the recent past.[28] Such overuse of antibiotics in the farming community results in antibiotic resistance, and is causing difficulty for doctors in treating disease.[29]

Starvation

Did you also know that 40,000 children die every day of starvation? Every two seconds, day and night, another child dies of starvation. An estimated 60,000,000 people starve to death every year! Yet 80% of corn and 95% of oats grown in the U.S. are used to feed livestock, and 40% of the world's grain is fed to livestock for meat consumption by First World countries.[30] It takes sixteen pounds of grain and soybeans to produce one pound of beef, which never reaches the Third World countries.[31] The amount of grain it would take to feed 8.7 billion people is eaten annually by the world's cattle,[32] and only those with enough money to buy the meat actually get fed from this grain. Lester Brown from the Overseas Development Council estimates that 60,000,000 people could be adequately fed by the excess grain (12 million tons) if Americans reduced their meat consumption by only 10%.[33,34]

Factory Farming

We must also take into account the conditions of today's factory farms, which produce the majority of meat sold today. Thousands of hens, cows, and pigs are frequently housed in pens where they cannot walk or even turn around, while being fed hormones and antibiotics to both boost their growth and prevent the diseases that run rampant from such crowded conditions. Nine million cows, calves, chickens, turkeys, and pigs are slaughtered for human consumption in America every day.[35]

Dairy cows are often confined to concrete feedlots, where they are fed hormones to increase milk production, causing painful infections, udders that sometimes drag to the ground, and other health issues. They are mechanically milked up to three times a day. Because of current milking methods, hormones, and other factors, the amount of milk per cow increased from 4,622 pounds annually in 1940 to 16,498 pounds annually in 1996.[36] Despite the fact that there are only approximately 9.4 million dairy cows today compared to 23.6 million in 1940, milk production has increased from 109 billion pounds in 1940 to an estimated 162 billion pounds in 2000.[37]

Calves raised for veal live a short and painful life. They are taken from their mother at birth and placed in a pen in which they cannot take a step or even lie down naturally. They are fed an anemia-producing diet that gives their meat the desired whitish-pink color of veal. After four months the animal is slaughtered and sold as veal. The meat is tender because the calf's muscles have never been used.[38]

Hens are kept in cages with no nests, and are crowded together so tightly that they have difficulty turning around or even lifting a wing.[39] They are fed hormones, which cause such rapid growth, their legs often cannot support their weight, and frequently have their beaks cut off, because they tend to harm one another in such crowded conditions. The barnyard chicken, with space to walk and a natural lifespan of 15-20 years is a far cry from today's factory "farm-raised" chickens, where an average of 80,000 are housed in one warehouse[40] and who have a lifespan of anywhere between two months (broilers) and 2 years (layers).[41]

A pig's life is no better than other factory raised animals. They are crowded in small pens where they can barely move, while being fed a diet that makes them gain weight more rapidly than their bone structure is able to handle. Hormones, antibiotics and other chemicals are regular additives to their feed, which frequently includes their own excrement and liquid wastes.[42] The majority of pigs raised on concrete or metal slats have damaged feet and legs due to constant pressure from the concrete floor or metal slats they have to stand on,[43] and a large percentage have pneumonia, stomach ulcers, or other health problems when they are slaughtered.[44]

Poor housing is not the only problem with our ever-growing addiction to meat. Use of natural resources and pollution are other mounting concerns. More than half of all water used in the United States is used in growing feed for livestock.[45] It takes 25 gallons of water to produce a pound of wheat and 2,500 gallons of water to produce a pound of meat.[46] Forests in America are being cleared at an astounding rate, the majority to produce grain for livestock.[47] For every eight acres of forest cleared in America, one is used for urban sprawl and the other seven are used for livestock production, both for growing livestock feed and grazing animals.[48] A person who consumes meat on a regular basis requires 3 1/2 acres of land for food production. A lacto-ovo vegetarian (eats dairy products and eggs) requires 1/2 acre, and a vegan (no animal products) requires only 1/6 of an acre.[49] Tropical rainforests are also being destroyed in devastating amounts to provide pasture for meat production.[50]

> *Do not be deceived: God cannot be mocked. A man reaps what he sows. The one who sows to please his sinful nature, from that nature will reap destruction; the one who sows to please the Spirit, from the Spirit will reap eternal life.*
> *Galatians 6:7-8*

Factory farms produce enormous amounts of animal waste, which emit toxic gasses into the air, such as ammonia, methane, and hydrogen sulfide. These gases frequently cause health issues for those on the farm and in the community, such as sore throats, headaches, skin rashes, infections, mental ailments, coughing, diarrhea, comas, seizures, and even death.[51,52,53] Runoff and leakage from the large waste lagoons, as well as the spraying of manure sends bacteria, nitrates, and dangerous microbes into the water supply, causing problems ranging from large-scale death of fish and excess algae growth to miscarriages and deaths in infants.[54] To bring this issue into perspective, consider that the total population of the United States produces 12,500 pounds per second of human waste and has a sewage system to deal with it. Livestock from the farms in America produce waste at the rate of 250,000 pounds per second, and there are no sewage systems to deal with the waste.[55] An estimated one billion tons of waste that is not recycled is produced annually from livestock.[56]

Caring for God's Creation

Aside from the fact that consuming excess meat is causing many kinds of sickness and disease, our addiction to meat has severe consequences on the world around us, from poor treatment of animals, to devastation of the environment, to millions of people dying of starvation. Sometimes we as Christians have a tendency to dismiss such topics as left-winged, earth-loving liberalism, but as Christians we have an obligation to care for God's creation to the best of our ability. The immense waste and destruction created by a meat-based diet is truly devastating. God has given us the role of stewards over His creation, and we must begin considering the effects of our decisions as they pertain not only to ourselves but also to those around us.

If you eat meat, eggs, or dairy products, consider purchasing grain fed, free roaming animals that have been raised on organic farms in a natural setting, and eating them less often. These animals have not been fed hormones, antibiotics, and grain with pesticides, and are much closer in nature to the clean animals spoken of in the Bible.

Deception at its Best

You may be wondering how we have come to believe that meat and dairy are health foods, when in fact, they are causing a host of diseases. Consider that the meat and dairy industries, along with the U.S. Department of Agriculture (USDA), have been responsible for the majority of nutritional education in American schools, and the answer is obvious. The USDA, whose original purpose was to support and promote the interests of farmers, is also responsible for setting nutritional guidelines, educating the public in these guidelines, and establishing food assistance programs.[57] If this is not a conflict of interest, I don't know what is. It would be difficult for the government to support the meat and dairy industries with taxpayer money while also exposing the whole truth about the nutritional devastation caused by eating meat and dairy.

The USDA financially supports the meat and dairy industries through buyouts which bolster prices, food assistance programs (15 of them), cash grants, the creation of the National Fluid Milk Processor Board to promote milk,[58] and by inflating prices the government pays for meat and dairy. The USDA purchases hundreds of millions of pounds of milk, cheese, and butter each year,[59] then uses these foods in the programs it has established from the National School Lunch Program to WIC (all with taxpayer dollars).

Despite the scientific evidence that dairy is hazardous to our health, the USDA continues to require that milk be included in the school lunch programs. Because of the USDA's divided interests in promoting the meat and dairy industries as well as defining the American public's dietary guidelines, which are taught everywhere from public schools to doctors' offices, Americans have been completely misinformed, lied to, and deprived of an honest dietary education. It isn't that the truth is impossible to come by— the problem is that the "experts" (medical doctors and school systems) are swayed by the propaganda of big industry and government combined. And who are we to question the "experts"?

Remember, an estimated 90% or more of all deaths in America are food-induced, primarily from eating an excess of meat and dairy products. We must learn the real truth from impartial sources. Getting a good and honest education in nutrition is one of the best things we can do for our families, friends, neighbors and a better and healthier America.

Chapter 6 Study Questions

1. List ten diseases or health disorders directly related to the consumption of meat.

   _____

   _____

   _____

   _____

   _____

2. What percentage of Americans die of Heart Disease?_____ Cancer? _____ Diabetes? _____

3. What are three results of the China-Cornell-Oxford Project that you found particularly interesting?

   _____

   _____

   _____

4. List ten diseases or health disorders that can be linked to consumption of dairy products.

   _____

   _____

   _____

   _____

   _____

5. Countries that consume the _____ animal
    products have the _____ rates of osteoporo-
    sis, and countries that consume the _____
    animal products have the _____ rates of
    osteoporosis.

    How does this information compare to what you have
    been taught regarding dairy products and osteoporosis?

    _____

    _____

    _____

6. What foods will supply your body with calcium without
    facilitating bone loss?

    _____

    _____

    _____

7. What is the recommended percentage of calories from
    protein? _____

    What plant foods can you eat to obtain this amount or
    more?

    _____

    _____

    _____

8. Can you get enough protein in your diet without eating animal products? _____

9. List three causes of concern related to meat-based diets other than disease.

   _____

   _____

   _____

10. What percentage of corn and oats grown in America are used to feed livestock? _____

11. _____ pounds of grain produce _____ pounds of beef.

12. _____ people die every year of starvation, _____% of Americans are dying of excess animal consumption, and we have a host of environmental issues related to meat production.

    Considering this information and other consequences of a meat-based diet, what are your thoughts?

    _____

    _____

    _____

    _____

    _____

13. How have most Americans come to believe that meat and dairy products are a necessary part of a healthy diet?

_____

_____

_____

14. Chapter 6 contained quite a bit of information, some of it possibly surprising. What three pieces of information affected you most?

_____

_____

_____

15. At this point, do you plan on making any changes in your current diet? _____

   If so, what?

_____

_____

_____

16. Bring your thoughts and feelings to the Lord, and ask for His wisdom and understanding in your diet and the role of animal products in particular.

Since we have these promises, dear friends, let us purify ourselves from everything that contaminates body and spirit, perfecting holiness out of reverence for God.
2 Corinthians 7:1

Chapter Seven

A Potpourri of Detrimental Foods

Do you not know that your body is a temple of the Holy Spirit,
who is in you, whom you have received from God?
You are not your own; you were bought at a price.
Therefore, honor God with your body.
1 Corinthians 6:19-20

There are a few other foods that play a major role in the diet of most Americans that are devastating to our bodies. Keep in mind God's design for our physical bodies, and how we have been swayed by the world's propaganda. Remember to consider the following information through the filter of Scripture rather than through the hazy lens of the world's perspective.

Refined Foods

We frequently hear that we need to limit our intake of refined or processed foods. Many people think of cookies, candy, and cakes as refined, and they definitely are. But most other foods you find on the grocery store shelves and in restaurants have also been refined. These refined foods have had many of their beneficial properties removed, have undergone processing, and are packaged in a form very different than the original food.

Common processed foods that you will find in the grocery store are breads, pastas, white rice, cookies, cakes, crackers, muffins, pretzels, candy, prepackaged meals, prepackaged snacks, canned foods, and condiments. Americans consume over 90% of their calories from refined foods and animal products.[1]

Manufacturers often remove beneficial parts of the ingredients, and then add in harmful substances such as salt, sugar, hydrogenated oil, preservatives, and food coloring. White bread and pasta are good examples of refined foods. The following nutrients found in the grain are missing in white bread and pasta:[2]

- 62% of the zinc
- 72% of the magnesium
- 95% of vitamin E
- 50% of the folic acid
- 72% of the chromium
- 78% of the vitamin B6
- 78% of the fiber

We need fiber and all of the other nutrients God created in foods. These are the foods God created for the fuel our bodies were made to run on. We would be foolish to think that we can tamper so greatly with our foods and not suffer health consequences. Refined foods are not proper nourishment for our bodies. When we eat them we are excluding the majority of vital nutrients, both known and unknown, contained in the original food.

Refined foods are linked to the following health issues: *oral cavity cancer, stomach cancer, colorectal cancer, intestinal cancer, breast cancer, thyroid cancer, respiratory tract cancer, diabetes, gall bladder disease, and heart disease.*[3] A study of 65,000 women over a period of six years showed that those who ate diets high in white bread, white rice, and pasta, were 2.5 times more likely to have type II diabetes, compared to the women whose diet was high in fiber-rich foods, such as whole wheat bread and brown rice.[4] In a nine-year study of 34,492 women from the ages of 55-69, the risk of death from heart disease in those eating refined grains was higher by two-thirds.[5]

How do you avoid buying and eating processed devitalized foods? When buying grain products, check the label and buy whole grain! Items labeled as "wheat bread, wheat bagel, grain bread," or "grain cereal" most likely contain white flour and other refined ingredients. Look for the words "whole wheat," "brown rice," or other names of whole grains as the first ingredient in the ingredient list. The word "enriched" on a label is just another way of saying the original beneficial ingredients have been removed, and synthetic vitamins and minerals have been added. It is impossible to replace all of the known and unknown nutrients that have been removed in the refining process, so eat whole foods: whole grains, whole grain breads, whole fruits, and whole vegetables. Aim at making your diet consist of 90% unrefined plant foods. Turn away from man's wisdom of refining food, and rely on God's wisdom, that He created the perfect foods to perfectly nourish our bodies. *"For the foolishness of God is wiser than man's wisdom, and the weakness of God is stronger than man's strength"* (1 Corinthians 1:25).

Life is more than food, and the body more than clothes.
Luke 12:23

Fats

Fats, like protein, are a necessary part of our diet. Americans, however they may try to stick to a low-fat diet, are deceived into believing that a typical "low-fat" diet of refined foods is a healthy one. Instead, this type of diet is lacking in vital nutrients and fiber and will not promote optimum health.

Eating whole grains, fresh vegetables, beans, fruits, and nuts will supply your body with adequate amounts of healthy oils (fats). Refined oils should be limited because of their high fat content, as well as the toxicity from heating oil to high temperatures. We need to consume the right types of fats from whole foods, and avoid the wrong types of fats (refined oils, hydrogenated oils, meat, cheese, milk).

It is best to avoid refined oils, but when you do consume them, choose those that are high in monounsaturated fats and low in polyunsaturated fats. *Avoid saturated, hydrogenated, and partially hydrogenated oils completely!* Check the foods you currently have in your refrigerator, cabinets, and pantry. How many contain saturated fat, hydrogenated, or partially hydrogenated oils? You may have more than you think. Most processed foods that seem to slip right into our pantry and cupboards contain these dangerous oils.

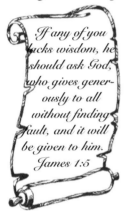

If any of you lacks wisdom, he should ask God, who gives generously to all without finding fault, and it will be given to him.
James 1:5

What is hydrogenated oil, and why is it so dangerous? Hydrogenation or partial hydrogenation is the process of turning liquid oil into a solid by adding hydrogen molecules to the oil. Hydrogenation creates trans fatty acids, which have the same effect in your body as saturated fats. Trans fatty acids cause all of the same diseases as fats from animal sources, such as cancer, heart disease, diabetes, and stroke. Some foods that may contain hydrogenated or partially hydrogenated oils are crackers, cookies, doughnuts, candy, French fries, frozen foods, boxed foods, breads, cereals, meal replacement bars, fruit snacks, cakes, pies, chips, etc. Begin reading labels and get rid of the hydrogenated and partially hydrogenated oils! They were not created to be digestible, only to make foods crisp and lengthen shelf-life … while shortening yours!

In summary, avoid processed oils, hydrogenated and partially hydrogenated oils, polyunsaturated oils, saturated oils, and animal products containing fat, such as meat and dairy products. Eat whole grains, vegetables, fruits, beans, nuts, and seeds to meet your daily need for good oils. When you use oil, choose olive or another beneficial oil such as Udo's Choice Oil Blend®. Those who are overweight should consume less oil, and those who are underweight or maintaining a good weight can have a little more. Avoid processed foods. They usually contain bad oils. Remember, foods in their most natural state are the healthiest!

Sodium

Sodium is a naturally occurring element in fresh raw fruits and vegetables. Our bodies require sodium, but not more than what is found naturally in fresh fruits and vegetables. Adding salt to your food is likely to increase development of disease in your body. Salt intake has been linked to high blood pressure, stomach cancer, and osteoporosis.[6] Adding excessive sodium to your food, according to a large study published in *The Lancet,* increases the risk of death, regardless of blood pressure or other factors.[7]

Refined foods are often dangerously high in sodium and should be avoided. Have you ever wondered why canned, boxed, and frozen foods are so high in sodium? The manufacturer has refined the foods so much, removing the natural goodness and flavor, that they must add salt and sugar to make them palatable! These are foods with very little to no nutritional benefit to your body. Try eating food as God created it, without excess salt added for flavor, and watch your taste buds adjust to the exciting varieties of foods God has created for us!

Sugar

Do you have a sweet tooth? If so, you're not alone. The average American consumes approximately 33 teaspoons of sugar each day, totaling 150 pounds per year! Sounds like a lot, doesn't it? Do you think you eat that much sugar daily? Take a look at the labels on the food you currently have in your home. "Sugar" is not the only way sugar is listed as an ingredient on a label. Here are a few others to look for: raw sugar, brown sugar, confectioner's sugar, powdered sugar, corn syrup, dextrose, sucrose, cane sugar, molasses, beet sugar, refined sugar, granulated sugar, turbinado sugar, honey, lactose, maltose, and fructose.

What is so bad about sugar? It doesn't have any fat, so what makes it unhealthy? Sugar is a refined substance that causes all kinds of problems in our bodies. It does not fill you up, and has no fiber or beneficial properties. Because it offers no nutritional value whatsoever and does not fill you up, a person who eats a lot of sugar still tends to eat plenty of other foods, and voila ... a spare tire around the waist!

Extra weight is not the only problem that comes from consuming refined sugar. Sugar is an addictive food; the more you eat, the more you want. Withdrawal symptoms are common when a person discontinues eating sugar, similar to giving up caffeine or any other drug. These include, but are not limited to, fatigue, depression, aching limbs, moodiness, and headaches.

Simple carbohydrates, refined sugar for example, do not fill you up. Your brain does not receive the message that your stomach is full; therefore, you can eat way too much sugar without receiving a warning signal to stop. Because of its refined nature, sugar is absorbed quickly into the bloodstream, causing a rapid rise in your blood-sugar level. Your pancreas then releases insulin to lower your blood-sugar, which drops it quickly to levels often below what you started with. When this reaction occurs, you feel tired, irritable, cranky, and hungry.

It's easier to go down a hill than up it, but the view is much better at the top.
Henry Ward Beecher

Complex carbohydrates are full of fiber and fill you up, and are processed slowly by your body. If you are in tune with your body, you will reach for a complex carbohydrate or protein—a piece of whole grain bread, bowl of brown rice or barley, or a handful of nuts. But usually the pattern is to drink a soda or grab another sugary snack and start the process all over again.

Following is a partial list of other health issues that can be related to sugar consumption. See if you recognize any of these in yourself or your children: *irritability, insomnia, suppressed immune system, loss of minerals from your body, hyperactivity, anxiety, crankiness, cancer, poor eyesight, hypoglycemia, acidic digestive tract, premature aging, tooth decay, obesity, arthritis, asthma, overgrowth of candida (yeast infection), gallstones, heart disease, appendicitis, multiple sclerosis, hemorrhoids, varicose veins, eczema, cataracts, emphysema, liver problems, kidney problems, headaches, migraines, pancre-*

atic damage, depression, Attention Deficit Hyperactivity Disorder (ADHD), kidney stones, PMS, chronic degenerative diseases, epileptic seizures, high blood pressure, and antisocial behavior.[8]

When it comes to sugar, stop the yo-yo effect! Choose whole grains, fresh fruits or vegetables, and raw nuts for a snack. Your blood sugar will remain balanced throughout the day, and you'll feel great without the ups and downs sugar provides. Your body (and likely your family and friends) will thank you for it!

Sugar Substitutes

If you think sugar is deceptively sweet, then sugar substitutes run away with the grand prize of deception! Sugar substitutes, including saccharin, aspartame, and sucralose, are anywhere from 200 to 1000 times sweeter than sugar. But reactions and side effects to these chemicals are less than sweet.

Saccharin

Saccharin, or benzoic sulphinide, the first artificial sweetener, was discovered in 1879. You know it as Sweet-n-Low. In 1991 the FDA began requiring the manufacturer of saccharin to carry a warning label stating that it causes cancer in laboratory animals. Saccharin is 200 times sweeter than sugar and is used in over 9,000 commercially packaged foods and beverages in place of sugar, in addition to table use.

Aspartame

Aspartame, commonly known as NutraSweet or Equal, was discovered in 1965 and approved in 1981. Aspartame is used in over 5,000 commercially packaged products, in addition to table use. Aspartame is perhaps the most dangerous artificial sweetener on the market today! It contains a combination of aspartic acid, phenylalanine, and methyl ester. Methanol (wood alcohol) is formed when methyl comes in contact with chymotrypsin in the small intestine. Methanol breaks down in the body into formaldehyde, a toxic chemical, and formic acid, which is the poison in the sting of fire ants. Aspartic acid and phenylalanine are amino acids present in other foods in conjunction with other amino acids. By themselves, however, they are neurotoxic. When aspartic acid and phenylalanine do not occur in a natural state with other amino acids, the body cannot process them properly.

Reactions to aspartame can occur immediately following ingestion or slowly over a period of years. Many people suffering from the side effects of ingesting this poison have baffled themselves and doctors with small to chronic conditions in which they cannot find the cause or cure. Methanol toxicity, or aspartame poisoning, can mimic, trigger, or worsen the following diseases: *fibromyalgia, arthritis, chronic fatigue syndrome, multiple sclerosis, Parkinson's disease, Epstein-Barr, lupus, epilepsy, hypothyroidism, diabetes, multiple chemical sensitivities, Lyme disease, Grave's disease, post-polio syndrome, lymphoma, panic disorder, Alzheimer's disease, non-Hodgekins, depression, and Attention Deficit Disorder.*[9,10]

But those who hope in the Lord will renew their strength. They will soar on wings like eagles; they will run and not grow weary, they will walk and not be faint.
Isaiah 40:31

There are a host of other side effects. Following is a partial list: *abdominal pain, anxiety, asthmatic reactions, bloating, fluid retention, hyperglycemia, hypoglycemia, confusion, memory loss, chest pains, slurring of speech, arthritis, muscle spasms, nausea, insomnia, irritability, dizziness, headaches, migraines, fatigue, hair loss, vision loss, hearing impairment, hyperactivity, tremors, restless legs, menstruation changes, PMS, excessive thirst, excessive hunger, birth defects, brain damage, seizures, convulsions, impotency, itching, and peptic ulcers.*[11,12]

Do you consume aspartame on a regular basis and have any of the above symptoms or other unexplainable symptoms? Aspartame is a deceptive substance. Aspartame, known as NutraSweet or Equal, is not a food at all, but a man made chemical that destroys our bodies.

Sucralose

Sucralose, commonly known as Splenda, is approximately 600 times as sweet as sugar. Sucralose, like other artificial sweeteners, is a chemical manufactured in a laboratory. Approved for consumption in 1998, Splenda has quickly become a favorite sweetener for many Americans. Why? Because consumers have been led to believe that sucralose is a natural form of sugar, without any calories. Its box says it is "made from sugar, so it tastes like sugar." What they don't tell you on the box is that sucralose is made from sugar and chlorine! Three atoms of chlorine are substituted on a sucrose molecule for three hydrogen-oxygen groups. Does this sound natural to you? Chlorine is a health hazard as well as a known carcinogen.

Sucralose is now common in many processed foods, such as cookies, cakes, baking mixes, other baked goods, sodas, sauces, syrups, jams, jellies, desserts, drink mixes, juices, chewing gum, and others. Many people use sucralose (Splenda) in their coffee, tea, other beverages, cooking, and baking on a regular basis.

Sucralose is among the least researched of all artificial sweeteners, but some side effects have already been documented in laboratory animals, including: *shrunken thymus glands, enlarged liver, enlarged kidneys, lymph follicle atrophy in spleen and thymus, decreased red blood cell count, miscarriage, decreased weight of unborn child, diarrhea, and others.*[13,14] Note that the thymus glands have been proven to shrink up to 40%. The thymus gland is the foundation and base of our immune system! No long-term studies have been done on the effects of sucralose consumption by humans.

Whole Foods are Key

In a world where low-fat, low-sugar, low-carb foods are heavily promoted, we can easily fall into the trap of seeing food as the world sees it, rather than how God created it. God created whole foods, with no chemical additives or alterations. His foods taste great just as they are! Some are high in fat, some high in sugar, and many high in carbohydrates, but they are whole foods that our bodies can process. These whole foods were created to be utilized by the human body. When we begin to remove parts of the food God created and add in our own man-made chemicals, we are not giving our bodies what God designed for them to receive for optimum health, and are actually harming them by ingesting foreign substances.

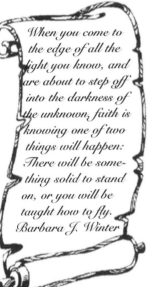

When you come to the edge of all the light you know, and are about to step off into the darkness of the unknown, faith is knowing one of two things will happen: There will be something solid to stand on, or you will be taught how to fly.
Barbara J. Winter

If you are eating man-made, processed, devitalized foods, whether or not you currently recognize any symptoms of ill-health, they are at work in your body. Diseases and medical conditions do not suddenly and mysteriously appear out of nowhere. Your body is like a machine that requires proper fuel and maintenance. If you have not been filling your tank with good whole foods, including grains, beans, vegetables, fruits, nuts, and seeds, but instead eating processed, canned, boxed, sugar-free, low-fat, low-carb foods, you can be sure that each cell in your body is becoming weaker, not stronger. These devitalized foods lead to disease, and the chemicals help speed up the process.

If you desire the sweetness of sugar, try eating sugar in its natural form—fresh fruits and dried fruits. Cut out all refined and processed sugars for a while, and definitely throw out the man-made sugar substitutes. Try it for a month and see how you feel! If you must use a sweetener in baking, your coffee or tea, or for other purposes, try stevia, or a more natural form of sugar such as honey, fructose, pure maple syrup, brown rice syrup, or Sucanat.® As a sugar alternative, stevia is an herb that has been reported to decrease hypertension, improve digestion, aide in weight loss, regulate blood sugar levels, and is safe for diabetics. Whatever you do, stick to God's foods in the most natural form He created them. [15,16]

Caffeine

Do you need your morning cup of coffee to get you going? How about in the afternoon as a pick-me-up? Caffeine is one of the most widely used addictive stimulants in America today. Even children are hooked on it. From sodas to coffee to chocolate, Americans rely on the caffeine in these foods to give them a boost.

Does caffeine have negative side effects and consequences for its users? Those who have tried to eliminate it from their diets will give you a resounding yes! Caffeine is an addictive drug, and those who consume it regularly suffer withdrawal symptoms when they don't consume it at expected times. Withdrawal symptoms include headache, moodiness, feelings of hunger, fatigue, and constipation.

Caffeine is a health hazard. Caffeine raises both blood pressure and cholesterol, and those who consume it on a regular basis have a higher risk of cardiac arrhythmias.[17] It is a stimulant that affects the nervous system, causing nervousness, anxiety, hyperactivity, and insomnia. Caffeine is a thief of good, deep, restful, and healing sleep, promoting disease by not giving your body proper time to heal and recover from the day's stresses. Caffeine increases a woman's risk of developing uterine fibroids and fibrocystic breasts,[18] and is a diuretic, causing loss of valuable minerals.

If you are hooked on caffeine and find yourself irritable, moody, nervous, or lethargic, consider what life would be like without the constant ups and downs you currently experience. What would it be like to have a restful night's sleep and begin your day rejuvenated without relying on that cup of coffee? After the withdrawal symptoms disappear (approximately four to five days), you will likely enjoy a much calmer yet naturally invigorating lifestyle without the ups and downs, irritability and sluggishness associated with caffeine consumption. If taste and having something warm in your tummy is an issue, switch to a natural coffee replacement or herbal tea. There is an abundance of delicious and healthy warm beverages you can enjoy as often as you desire.

Chapter 7 Study Questions

1. What are refined foods?

   _____

   _____

   _____

2. Why are refined foods unhealthy?

   _____

   _____

   _____

3. List five refined foods that you have in your refrigerator, pantry, or cupboards.

   _____

   _____

   _____

   _____

4. What is hydrogenated oil, and why is it so dangerous?

   _____

   _____

   _____

5. List three products in your home that contain hydrogenated or partially hydrogenated oil.

_____

_____

_____

6. What are some other names for "sugar"?

_____

_____

_____

7. Do you or does anyone you know experience any of the side effects of sugar consumption? If so, which ones?

_____

_____

_____

8. Name the three most widely used sugar substitutes.

_____

_____

_____

9. What are some of the dangers of consuming artificial sweeteners?

    _____

    _____

    _____

10. Caffeine is one of the most widely used

    _____ _____

    in America today.

11. What are some of the side effects of caffeine?

    _____

    _____

    _____

12. Do you regularly consume any of the food items covered in chapter 7? If so, which ones?

    _____

    _____

    _____

13. What percentage of your diet is made up of refined foods? _____ Meat or dairy products? _____ Whole foods (vegetables, fruits, grains, beans, etc.)?

    _____

14. Consider the health benefits of adding whole foods and removing harmful refined foods and other dangerous food substances from your diet. How do you think your body would benefit from these changes? Ask the Lord for strength and wisdom in implementing a healthy diet and lifestyle. This is a great time to find a friend who is on the same path as you want to be on. Begin to share and encourage one another in the things of God, including making healthy food choices.

_____

_____

_____

_____

_____

_____

Be joyful in hope, patient in affliction,
faithful in prayer.
Romans 12:12

Chapter Eight

Beating Disease: A Positive Prognosis

Heal the sick, raise the dead, cleanse those who have leprosy,
drive out demons. Freely you have received, freely give.
Matthew 10:8

What is the standard American diet, and why is it causing so much sickness and disease? Is there any hope if you already have a serious health condition or disease? We have already covered what is healthy for your body, and some of the foods that are killing us. But what are we *really* eating? Are we eating enough of the healthful foods, and little enough of the harmful foods to maintain a healthy body free of sickness and disease?

Following the Food Guide Pyramid (the foods and proportions recommended by the USDA) actually causes the diseases we are trying to avoid! The USDA recommends in the Food Guide Pyramid that we eat 4-6 servings a day of milk, yogurt, cheese, meat, poultry, fish, dry beans, eggs, and nuts. Considering that most of these are animal products, Americans are in dietary trouble if they follow this eating plan. The USDA also recommends in the Pyramid that we eat 8-11 servings of bread, cereal, rice, and pasta. This would be fantastic if all of the carbohydrates they recommend are whole grain, but there are no such specifications, and the pictures show otherwise. The Pyramid also recommends that 5-8 servings of fruits and vegetables should be eaten, but with no distinction made between fresh, raw, steamed, canned, frozen, or fried. Considering all of the studies available and the material we have covered thus far, we know that a diet based on refined foods and animal products causes and worsens sickness and disease.

It's bad enough that this information is taught in our schools and other public arenas, but what's even worse is that this is the goal many Americans feel they should try to achieve! I say "try" to achieve, because while many make this their goal, they fall short in the beneficial categories, while consuming more than the allotted amount of potentially harmful foods. According to Joel Fuhrman, M.D., in *Eat to Live*, 50% of all Americans do not eat any fruit at all on a given day, and 50% of Americans do not eat even three servings of vegetables a day. The vegetable category even includes French fries and potato chips![1]

This is the confidence we have in approaching God: that if we ask anything according to his will, he hears us. And if we know that he hears us—whatever we ask—we know that we have what we asked of him.
1 John 5:14-15

Americans as a whole seem to be falling very short in eating disease-preventing foods, while overloading on refined foods, meat, and dairy. Fifty-one percent of all calories consumed by Americans come from refined and processed foods, 42% from dairy and animal products, and only 7% of all calories eaten by Americans come from vegetables and fruits. Once again this includes even unhealthy French fries as a vegetable.[2]

Are you an average American when it comes to eating? What do you purchase at the grocery store, feed your family at home, and eat when you are in a restaurant? Now is the time to open up your refrigerator, pantry, and cupboards, and take an inventory. Go ahead! This is a true test of where you really are in your family's eating habits. Pull out a few items: crackers, mayonnaise, pasta, boxed dinners, canned veggies—whatever you have sitting on your shelves. Now begin reading the labels. Do you see any of the items that are causing health problems for most Americans: refined flour, hydrogenated oil, sugar, sodium, dairy, additives, preservatives, food colorings, etc.? Don't forget to check your freezer. Some of the worst food products can be hidden here: foods full of animal protein, hydrogenated oil, sodium, sugar, and other harmful ingredients. Remember, if you can't easily read the ingredients, most likely they are not good for you!

For God did not give us a spirit of timidity, but a spirit of power, of love and of self-discipline. 2 Timothy 1:7

What do you and your family typically eat in a day? Does your diet consist primarily of these refined foods that are in your pantry, or does it consist primarily of fresh vegetables and fruits, whole grains, beans, nuts, and seeds? Be honest with yourself! What percentage of these healthful foods make up your diet? Ten percent, 20%, 30%, 50%, 70%? Most experts in the field of nutrition and disease reversal recommend that your diet consist of 90% unrefined plant based foods. If you are sick or just feeling sluggish, consider the proportion of unrefined plant-based foods you are eating versus refined foods or animal products.

If you went through the above exercise with me, I want to congratulate you! Coming to terms with where you really are is the first and biggest step to gaining a truly healthy and vibrant body. If you have very few refined foods in your home, great job! Keep it up! I want to encourage you to continue on the road to good health by continuing to learn and share your knowledge and success with others. Encourage and help those around you who are willing to change their way of eating to a healthy and life-giving diet.

If you had less than desirable results, don't despair! Be encouraged that you have taken the first step by taking the time to learn about true health and wellness. Thank God now for the wonderful human body he created for you to serve Him in. Let Him know how appreciative you are for Him creating a body that strives to maintain health. Thank Him because you do not have to be fearful of sickness and disease.

Can Diseases Be Reversed?

What if you are already sick? What if you have a disease that has taken over your life? Is there hope? Yes, yes, yes!!! Many doctors are now accomplishing disease reversal through proper nutrition. Time and time again they have proven that when you remove harmful foods from your diet, and eat a diet rich in plant foods full of vital nutrients, your body responds almost immediately! Over time, old weak cells replace themselves with new, stronger cells, and bit-by-bit your body rebuilds itself into a new strong, healthy, and disease free body. It does take time, but good results are so motivating they can throw you into a whole new way of life, and a new way of thinking!

We have already established that almost all disease is caused by or made worse by the foods we eat. Let's take a quick look at some of the main killer diseases, and how food affects them.

Heart Disease

Heart disease is the leading cause of death in America, accounting for over 50% of all deaths in the United States.[3] According to many experts, it is not only avoidable, but also reversible. This is great news for all of us! Most Americans have lived the majority of their lives eating a diet high in animal protein, fat, and refined carbohydrates. The majority of Americans who eat animal products have issues relating to heart disease, and most don't even know it. Fifty percent of all Americans will die of heart disease. Forty percent of children from ages 4-11 already show signs of heart disease, according to Joel Fuhrman, M.D., in his book *Eat to Live*.[4] Fat and cholesterol build up and coat arteries no matter what the age of the person consuming it.

A cheerful look brings joy to the heart, and good news gives health to the bones.
Proverbs 15:30

The good news is that when a person stops eating a diet high in animal products and refined foods, and instead eats a diet rich in plant-based foods, heart disease actually reverses itself and disappears. Many people will be skeptical of such information that may sound over-simplistic. If medical doctors cannot stop heart disease from advancing, how can ordinary people who simply change their diet? It really is very simple when you think about it. God created our bodies and gave us the proper foods to enable them to function at an optimum level. We choose what we put into our bodies. The foods we eat bring life and health, or sickness and death. Heart disease is the number one killer, and according to many experts, an avoidable and reversible disease.

> *Every tomorrow has two handles. We can take hold of it with the handle of anxiety or the handle of truth.*
> *Henry Ward Beecher*

Remember that eating the foods God created in the form He created them is one of the most important things you can do for your health. Trying not to exceed the limits of the so-called experts will not do you much good when it comes to disease reversal. The American Heart Association recommends eating no more than 30% of your total calories as fat. But according to studies, the majority of patients on the American Heart Association diet with heart disease continue to become worse. No studies have shown that the diet the American Heart Association advocates halts or reverses heart disease.[5] Eating whole foods such as vegetables, fruits, beans, and grains, without adding animal products, allows your blood to thin, your arteries to clear, and a new and healthier you!

Cancer

Cancer will take the lives of approximately 38% of all Americans[6] and is the second leading cause of death in America![7] Once again, according to experts, it is avoidable and frequently reversible. Americans are fearful of cancer. Most of us have a friend, acquaintance, or family member who has battled cancer, which is a dreaded disease largely because of its ambiguity. It seems to be a disease that we have no control over, and once it is detected, the treatment can be just as scary and harmful as the cancer itself.

With all of the money being spent on cancer research over the last thirty years, one might assume the research scientists are close to finding a cure for cancer. At least you might expect them to have a good understanding of what causes cancer and how to avoid it. In the last thirty years, over $35 billion of federal money has been spent on cancer research (this figure does not include private money). Over $1 trillion has been spent on medical treatment for cancer,[8] yet incidences and deaths resulting from cancer or the treatment thereof are rising significantly. The American Cancer Society estimates that 570,280 Americans will die of cancer in this year alone!

Let's take breast cancer as an example. More women get breast cancer than any other type of cancer. Approximately 185,000 American women are diagnosed every year with breast cancer, and approximately 46,000 do not survive. Every twelve minutes, twenty-four hours a day, another woman dies from breast cancer.

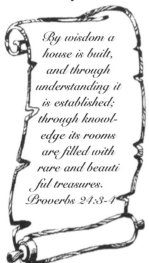

By wisdom a house is built, and through understanding it is established; through knowledge its rooms are filled with rare and beautiful treasures.
Proverbs 24:3-4

These statistics are almost identical for men with prostate cancer. Every minute of every day and every night, another person dies from some form of cancer.[9]

The statistics sound dismal, and the medical community is not offering much help. Is there hope, and is there a solution? The answer can be found, but outside of the medical community's method of early detection and harmful forms of treatment. God fashioned our bodies in a way that they consistently rebuild to create and maintain health. When we look at the foods God created our bodies to thrive on and how they build healthy cells, we gain insight not only into health but sickness and disease.

Food is the building block for each and every one of the one hundred trillion cells in your body. Each day billions of cells die and your body creates new cells to replace them. The strength and health of your cells depends upon their building blocks.

Let's look at what cancer really is, and how it can be avoided and even reversed when your body is given proper and ample nutrition. Cancer, simply put, is a cell that has malfunctioned, and is no longer under the direction of the brain. Cancer cells were once regular cells in the body that no longer behave like normal cells. Instead they multiply rapidly and wreak havoc on your system. You may be surprised to know that most people have some of these "maverick" cells somewhere in their body at any given point in time, but your immune system quickly identifies them and removes them from your body.

Do not be anxious about anything, but in everything, by prayer and petition, with thanksgiving, present your requests to God. And the peace of God, which transcends all understanding, will guard your hearts and your minds in Christ Jesus. Philippians 4:6-7

What causes your normal healthy cells to become dysfunctional and even harmful to your body? Experts believe it is a combination of an accumulation of toxins and a lack of vital nutrients. In essence, we are feeding ourselves poison and starving our bodies of necessary nutrients to maintain health. Toxins accumulate in our bodies from outside sources such as air pollution and chemicals we come in contact with, but the majority of damage is caused by what we actually ingest. Animal products, preservatives, man-made chemicals labeled as food, refined food products, and other food sources are just some of the things we ingest that actually harm rather than build our cells. As much as we eat, our bodies can still be lacking in vital nutrients necessary for building healthy cells. Eating an ample amount of fresh fruits, vegetables, beans, and grains, while limiting animal products, is the key to good health.

Knowing what you now know about cancer, consider the medical approach to alleviating it. Does it make sense, if your body was created to heal itself when given ample nutritional fuel, to attack the cancer with surgery, chemotherapy, radiation and other destructive measures, or to build the body's natural defenses so it can fight the cancer on its own? Cancer cells will die off when they are not fed. Cleansing the body of toxins and feeding it an abundant amount of nutrients will allow it to heal and rid itself of destructive cancer cells.

> *As I see it every day you do one of two things: build health or produce disease in yourself.*
> *Adelle Davis*

Cancer does not attack quickly. It takes years for cancer cells to divide and multiply. The problem is we think we don't have cancer until it has been detected, and by then it has spent years in the body multiplying and wreaking havoc. According to Harvey Diamond in Fit for Life, a New Beginning, cancer cells must grow and multiply for about 10 years to become the size of a pea and actually be detectable.[10] Even then, unless you have reason to have a screening or you detect a lump yourself, you may not know you have cancer.

What should we do? Accept the fact that all of us are subject to getting sick if we don't give our bodies what they need to be healthy. Begin now by refreshing your body with vital nutrients from fresh vegetables, fruits, beans, and grains, and cut out the harmful foods and beverages. You are likely to notice a significant difference in how you look and feel, and you will be encouraged that your body is rebuilding stronger, healthier cells. No one needs to live in fear of cancer. Cancer requires toxins and a lack of nutrients to develop. Feed your body healthy foods, and it will produce healthy cells.

Diabetes

Diabetes is reported as the fourth leading cause of death from disease in America,[11] and is perhaps one of the most misunderstood and underestimated diseases in today's culture. Yet the general population does not know what causes it or how to avoid it. Over 6% of the American population has diabetes.[12] It is difficult to know how many deaths are caused by diabetes, because only 10-15% of those people who have diabetes have listed it as the primary cause of death on their death certificates.[13] The effects of diabetes are absolutely devastating, and can include, but are not limited to, *heart disease, stroke, high blood pressure, kidney disease, pregnancy complications, blindness, nervous system disease, amputations, dental disease, and biochemical imbalances.*[14]

While Type I diabetes (child onset) can frequently be managed by proper diet, Type II diabetes (adult onset) can usually be reversed and cured, frequently within a short amount of time. With Type I diabetes, there is actually a problem with the pancreas, where it does not secrete enough insulin. A person with this condition, however, can still benefit greatly from the same diet that reverses and cures a person with Type II diabetes.

Type II is the most prevalent form of diabetes. It is completely preventable, and in most cases completely reversible. So what causes diabetes, and how can we avoid it? Many people believe that it is caused from eating excess sugar or from the pancreas producing a lack of insulin, but this is not the case. Having excess fat in the blood, which coats the cells, in addition to eating a diet high in refined foods, causes diabetes. When sugar enters the bloodstream, the pancreas produces insulin to normalize the blood-sugar level. If there is excess fat, however, the insulin is not able to reach the cells, and the blood sugar level becomes dangerously high. The problem typically is not due to a lack of insulin, but because there is too much fat for the body to be able to utilize the insulin it does produce. Being overweight by only ten to twenty pounds can significantly alter your cells ability to absorb and utilize insulin.

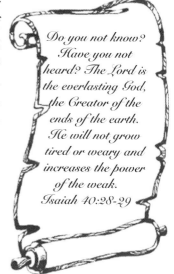

Do you not know? Have you not heard? The Lord is the everlasting God, the Creator of the ends of the earth. He will not grow tired or weary and increases the power of the weak.
Isaiah 40:28-29

This is exciting news for diabetics, those who are told they are at risk for diabetes, and the general population! The diet that protects us from developing diabetes is the same diet that reverses it, and is the same diet that protects us from other diseases as well. More than 70% of Type II diabetics die of heart disease and strokes.[15] It would make sense, therefore, to eat a heart healthy diet if you have diabetes. It is beneficial for those with diabetes and those who want to avoid it to eat a diet particularly high in fiber and nutrient-rich foods, abundant in green vegetables and beans, while avoiding all animal products and refined foods. It is important for a person with diabetes to avoid all fruit juices and sugary vegetable juices, as well as dried fruits and all refined foods, including white bread, white rice, and white pasta.[16]

It is extremely important if you are diabetic and are considering making changes to your diet, that you do so under the care of your physician. Your blood sugar levels will change as your body becomes healthier from your new diet, and it is likely that your doctor will need to adjust your medication.

Final Thoughts

There are many other diseases we could cover, but the information would be similar regarding the majority of them. Diet is the best place to start in disease prevention and reversal. Man-made medication, surgery, and other medical procedures do not remove the cause of the illness, and frequently do not remove the illness itself. There are often supplements that can be beneficial to a person suffering from a particular illness, but first consider the foods you are eating and those you are not eating. Be sure you are well nourished as you add any supplements that may benefit your body, and don't count on supplements or medical treatment to make up for poor eating habits or a destructive lifestyle.

Consider how God made your body in His likeness. It is a truly magnificent piece of work, unique in so many ways, yet formed in God's image. Trust God that He will work in you as He has already begun, and ask Him to show you His best for you. Purpose to live in God's presence through the power of the Holy Spirit in all areas of your life, including choosing the foods you eat. God is so good to meet us where we are, and so merciful when we have lived in ways that are not His best for us. If you suffer from any disease,  illness, or other medical condition, and you need a touch from God, or just want to rededicate yourself to Him, will you pray with me now?

Our Dear Heavenly Father,

Lord, I love you. I love you even more than myself, more than my desires, my plans, and my dreams. I want with all my being to live for you, not only in things that seem important to me, but in things that are important to you. Lord, please forgive me for focusing on what I want, and choosing to ignore some of the best that you have brought me. Please grant me wisdom in all things, and understanding of your perfect will.

I dedicate myself to you now—my physical body, my heart, my soul, and my spirit. They are instruments for your purpose, and may they always be used accordingly. I pray that you would work in me and change me from the inside out. May I be a motivator for others who want to follow you. I rejoice in your ways, and choose to live out all that you show me day by day. Give me grace, strength, and joy as I take the path less traveled.

In Jesus' Name,
Amen

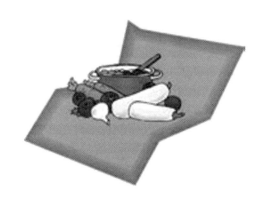

Chapter 8 Study Questions

1. Explain the Food Guide Pyramid and why it is faulty.

   _____

   _____

   _____

   _____

   _____

   _____

2. What are some of the main causes of heart disease?

   _____

   _____

   _____

3. When you stop eating a diet high in animal products and refined foods, and instead eat a diet rich in unrefined plant foods, heart disease actually _____

   _____.

   Whether or not you have been diagnosed with high blood pressure, high cholesterol, or other symptoms of heart disease, why not try a diet rich in plant foods and low in animal products, and see what great ways your body responds?

4. What is the second leading cause of death in America?

   _____

5. Do you personally know someone who has had cancer? Describe their experience.

   _____

   _____

   _____

   _____

   _____

   _____

6. What is cancer?

   _____

   _____

   _____

7. Can cancer be avoided? _____ How?

   _____

   _____

   _____

8. What are some of the health issues associated with diabetes?

   _____

   _____

   _____

9. What causes diabetes?

   _____

   _____

   _____

10. What type of diet protects against diabetes?

    _____

    _____

    _____

11. What piece of information in Chapter 8 surprised you
    the most?

    _____

    _____

    _____

12. What are your thoughts on the information in Chapter 8 and how it applies to you and your family?

_____

_____

_____

_____

_____

_____

13. What plans does the Lord have for you? What has He called you to do? Can you fulfill His purposes wholeheartedly now, and will you be able to do so in the future if you continue in the lifestyle you currently live?

_____

_____

_____

_____

_____

_____

14. Would you benefit from increasing your energy level, losing weight, or getting rid of headaches and other physical pain?

   _____

   Would you like to be able to keep up with your kids or come home from work and not be exhausted at the end of the day?

   _____

   How would your life be different if you were truly healthy?

   _____

   _____

   _____

15. Seek the Lord and make a commitment to Him to follow His ways in the both the physical and spiritual realms. Hosea 4:6a says, *"My people are destroyed from lack of knowledge."* Let us not be destroyed from lack of knowledge or from failing to apply the knowledge we have. Commit now to make the necessary changes in order to avoid sickness and maintain a healthy, vibrant body.

If you are willing and obedient,
you will eat the best from the land.
Isaiah 1:19

Chapter Nine

An Appetizing First Course Toward Healthy Living

Dear friend, I pray that you may enjoy good health and that all may go well with you, even as your soul is getting along well.
3 John 2

*A*re you asking yourself, "Where do I start?" Then let's begin the great adventure of learning how to implement a healthy lifestyle! First, there are a few basics to cover, and then you will be on your way to a lifetime of good health!

Let's Get Started

So far we have discussed foods that are good for us, and others that are bad for us, but we have not addressed what happens to all of the bad foods that have already entered our bodies. Where did they go? Did all of the destructive substances leave our bodies as they should have, or are there some still in there?

Our cells absorb both toxins and nutrients as our bodies process the food we eat and the air we breathe. The quality of the air we breathe, food we eat, and water we drink, however, determines our degree of health and our body's ability to release toxins. If a cell has effective building blocks, it will build with nutrients and release the toxins. However, if it cannot obtain the nutrients it requires to function at its best, many of the toxins that enter our bodies will not be discarded. Disease begins to occur at the cellular level when a cell does not have the nutrients it needs to function properly, and it holds onto toxins that should be released.

The first step in improving your health is to eliminate as many toxins and poisons as possible. Consider what you eat, drink, and breathe. Eliminating the destructive foods discussed previously is a great way to begin. By taking this step and drinking plenty of fresh clean water, your body will begin to release toxins and start building new, healthy cells. But there is much more you can do.

After years of eating foods that are actually destructive to your body, a good cleansing of your insides is a great idea. There are many ways to detoxify your body. The type and length of cleanse you choose will depend on your eating habits and your current level of health. Cleansing with the change of seasons is always a good idea. You will feel refreshed, renewed, revived, and invigorated.

First Things First

Americans tend to eat foods that do not easily move through the digestive system—foods that are low in fiber and high in fat. Do you remember making paper mache' as a child? Mix some white flour, water, and salt, and you have paste. The fiberless paste that we call white bread does not move through your intestines very well. Food containing little to no fiber actually stays in your intestines so long that it becomes impacted on your intestinal walls, forming a thick coating that becomes a toxic lining. The nutrients from the foods you eat or drink have to sift through this toxic lining to get into your bloodstream and reach your cells. In the process, some of the poisons from this lining get absorbed into your bloodstream. Yuk! This lining is also a breeding ground for parasites, yeast, fungi, and other creatures. Have you ever set a piece of meat in a warm moist environment for several days? What happens? It spoils! The food of a person eating the standard American diet usually takes between 72-96 hours to leave the body, when it should be eliminated within 24 hours.[1]

The result of this slow passage through our digestive systems, is that the average American has six to ten pounds of fecal matter stored in their colon.[2] Is it any wonder that we have so many problems with diverticulosis, diverticulitis, colon cancer, Crohn's disease, colitis, irritable bowel syndrome, and constipation? And these are just the obvious problems! All of the organs found near or next to the intestines are also affected, as well as every cell in your body which receives nutrients and/or toxins from your colon.

Good functioning of the bowel is so important that the first thing you should do is clean it out! At the same time, begin filling your body with valuable nutrients from fresh foods and juices to revitalize your cells. No matter what problems you are having, even if they seem unrelated to your colon, clean your colon first. After cleansing your colon, you will feel so much lighter and healthier. You may even notice that your stomach is flatter, your skin is clearer, and other health issues that have plagued you may begin to disappear. If you have had a difficult time losing weight, cleansing your colon can give you a jump-start.

Therefore encourage one another and build each other up, just as in fact you are doing. 1 Thessalonians 5:11

Many people today are uncomfortable discussing the bowel, and that is part of our problem. When a baby is born, what do you look for? The child must have a bowel movement or there is something very wrong. Doctors wait for it. Parents watch for it. Then as babies grow and begin to eat, we are delighted if their diapers are stinky only once a day, and easy to clean up!

So let's discuss healthy bowel movements for a moment. Healthy bowel movements should come two to four times a day, easily, without a lot of pushing, and they should be soft and unformed, like peanut butter or soft serve ice cream.[3] This type of bowel movement is the result of eating a diet that is high in fiber, and low in animal products and refined foods.

If our bodies should be producing two to four bowel movements a day, then Americans are falling extremely short. It is estimated that the average American falls short in the number of bowel movements by about 70,000 in their lifetime.[4] It's no wonder we are so sick! Food remains in the colon days longer than it should, and not all of it is being eliminated. The toxins from the food that is rotting in your colon are being absorbed into your bloodstream and carried to all of the cells in your body. If you want to have a healthy body, cleansing your colon and eating a diet high in fiber and plant foods is a must.

In addition to cleansing your colon, there are many other ways to cleanse your body. Raw food fasts, juice fasts, water fasts, and herbal supplement cleanses are all good ways to flush toxins from your body. Just remember to have a clean colon in good working order before you start.

One important thing to be aware of is the initial effect that cleansing has on a body filled with toxins. When toxins are being released from your cells into your body, you are likely to experience some uncomfortable symptoms such as tiredness, headaches, irritability, acne, or a feeling that you are "coming down with something." Just know that toxins are leaving your body, and that in a short amount of time you will feel better than before. You are cleansing your way to a new and healthier you!

If you would like to learn more about the benefits and process of healing your body through nutrition and cleansing, there are several great books on my recommended reading list. For specific cleansing information, refer to the books by Dr. Richard Schulze.

Exercise

How do you feel? And I mean it! How do you really feel right now? Are you tired or overweight? Do you have some physical problems that cause you to be more likely to lead a sedentary lifestyle? Do you ever sit at the park and watch children (or adults) play, and not even think of getting up to join them? Do you jump at the chance to walk a couple of miles or do some vigorous outdoor work, or would you prefer to pack a picnic lunch and sit at the park (or just stay home)? How would you describe your energy level today?

What should you do besides eating good, nourishing, healthy foods to obtain a healthy, vibrant body? You've got it! Exercise. I know you've heard it before, but I hope now you will begin to understand the true importance that exercise plays in the overall health of your body, and find a method of exercise that works for you!

Moderate exercise provides your cells with plenty of oxygen, increases your metabolism, improves the functioning of your immune system, and increases your energy level. It can also decrease your appetite and your body weight, slow the aging process, decrease stress, anxiety, and depression, improve your mood and promote a sense of well being.[5]

Steady, moderate exercise on a regular schedule is better than occasional heavy exercise, or yo-yo exercise—starting and stopping exercise programs. When you exercise moderately, walking 30-60 minutes a day, for example, your metabolism increases. With a higher metabolism, your body burns calories faster, even while resting.[6] You will also have more energy, allowing you to accomplish more throughout the day with less effort.

If you are the type of person that could use more energy throughout the day, regular exercise may give you exactly what you are looking for. It may be difficult to believe that using energy will give you energy, but you will be amazed at the difference after just a week or two of regular exercise. If you think you don't have the time to exercise, consider that you cannot have a healthy body without it. God created us to be active, to work, and to use the muscles He has given us (Genesis 3:23). Getting enough exercise in today's society can be difficult unless we make the effort to do so. Exercise should be just as much of a priority as providing healthy nourishing foods for our bodies. If we want to lead

We never repent of having eaten too little.

Thomas Jefferson

long productive lives, we must keep our bodies active and avoid sedentary lifestyles that are so common today.

Make it Work for You

What type of exercise is best for you? The best form of exercise is the one you will stick to. If being around other people motivates you, and you like to get out, then joining a gym may be for you. For others a gym might not be practical or sound at all appealing. Perhaps you enjoy spending time outdoors and would much prefer to walk around your neighborhood or local park. Many parks have hiking trails that make exercise even more enjoyable for those who love nature.

If you have small children, you have the added challenge of a few extra feet running around, and frequently have less solitary time available. For those of you with young children, it is highly beneficial to plan a set time for your exercise and make it a priority. You will make up for the time with added vitality and health. Here are some practical options for planning a regular exercise time:

- ◆ If your children are young enough to ride in a stroller, you can take walks and get plenty of exercise, while allowing your children to get some fresh air and sunshine.
- ◆ Frequently young children can keep up on a riding toy better than if they are walking. Big Wheels, bikes, and bikes with training wheels can be good options.
- ◆ Is there a time each day when your husband is home and can watch the children while you spend some time alone? If so this is a perfect time to take a walk or do whatever exercise you have planned. I frequently walk early in the morning before my husband leaves the house. Just roll out of bed, put on some sweats, stretch, and head out. This is also a *wonderful* time to commune with God. You will be amazed at what a difference it makes to start your day in the fresh open

air, alone with God! Later in the day or evening you can take a pleasure walk with your husband and kids. They need exercise too! Evening walks work as well. Whatever fits your schedule is what works best for you.

◆ Trading childcare with a neighbor for 45 minutes of exercise can be a great idea.

◆ Going to a gym or aerobic class that offers childcare works for those who love to get out.

◆ Exercise videos or exercise equipment such as a stationary bike, ski machine, rowing machine, or mini-trampoline can all be great ways to exercise at home.

Whatever you do, choose something you can stick with. Make a commitment, and hold fast to it!

Remember that a healthy lifestyle is just that—a lifestyle. Daily activities and habits form our lifestyle. Make exercise a part of your life, and make it a priority. Walk whenever possible. When you are out running errands, park far away and walk briskly in the parking lot. Take the stairs, pick up a sport you have always wanted to play, or just go outside and play with your children. Don't be lazy! Remember the benefits of exercise, and make it a part of your daily life.

Water

We couldn't discuss proper nutrition without giving water part of the spotlight. Your body is composed of approximately 70% water. Seventy-five percent of your muscle tissues, 80% of your lungs, 80.5 % of your brain, 95.5% of saliva, and 90.7% of your blood is made up of water.[7] Water is necessary for *all* body functions. From the time you put food into your mouth until the time it leaves your body, water is utilized in every part of the digestion process. Water transports nutrients to their proper destinations and carries wastes and toxins out of the body through the bowels, bladder, lungs, and skin.[8] Water also helps regulate your body temperature and performs many other bodily functions.

With water playing such an important role, we should make absolutely sure we drink plenty of pure, clean water. Much of our groundwater, however, is contaminated with pesticides, fertilizers, inorganic minerals, and many different chemicals. Our drinking water has been treated with even more chemicals, many of which are poisonous to our bodies.

We drink an average of 4,500 gallons of water in our lifetime! These 4,500 gallons contain approximately 200-300 pounds of rock (inorganic minerals), some of which stay in your body and settle in your joints, kidneys, arteries, gallbladder, and other areas where liquids flow.[9] Your body cannot utilize inorganic minerals found in the ground and drinking water; many are discarded, but the rest are distributed throughout your body. Drinking inorganic minerals and expecting your body to process them is similar to chewing on a handful of dirt or finely ground rocks, and expecting your body to benefit from ingesting them. The beneficial minerals that our bodies can utilize are those that plants have taken and utilized from the soil. When plants utilize minerals from the ground, they become organic minerals that our bodies can use and process.

The Lord God took the man and put him in the garden of Eden to work it and take care of it. Genesis 2:15

Typical municipal drinking water that has been processed contains inorganic minerals plus hundreds of chemicals. Polluted water pollutes your body! If you want to be healthy, you must consume fresh clean water, free of chemicals. Distilled water is your best choice. The water has been steamed and all of the impurities left behind. All you have left is fresh, pure water.

Drinking water throughout the day is a wonderful way to wash the toxins and impurities from your body, and it is necessary for achieving a healthy body. Drink a glass of water when you wake up, throughout the day, and 30 minutes before each meal. Try not to drink during a meal, as water dilutes the digestive juices, making digestion more difficult. Drinking fresh fruit and vegetable juices and eating high water-content fruits and vegetables are also very beneficial to your body.

Why Juice?

If God created fruits and vegetables as whole entities, why would we want to drink the juice and leave the pulp? Many people, including bottled juice drinkers, ask this question of those who consume freshly extracted vegetable and fruit juices. The answer is quite simple. Raw food has much more nutritional value than cooked food, but even with raw food, only 1-35% of the nutrients reach cell level.[10] If our bodies were in perfect health without the assault from bad food and environmental factors we currently face, then merely eating our vegetables would be fine. But we are not in perfect health, and we are constantly in contact with environmental toxins. Many people today are concerned (and rightly so) that they are not getting enough vitamins, minerals, and other vital nutrients from their diet alone. This is especially the case if you are eating the standard American diet of cooked food, fast food, and refined food. Most Americans do not consume enough raw fruits and vegetables to combat disease.

Raw vegetable juice provides a power packed punch of vitamins, minerals, and other nutrients in the organic form God created them. Because there is no fiber and the juice does not have to undergo a long digestive process, the nutrients from the juice reach your cells quickly and easily. In fact, when you drink pure vegetable juice, your body assimilates up to 92% of the nutrients.[11] These nutrients are fresh from the original source in greater quantities than could be consumed from the fruits or vegetables themselves. Can you imagine sitting down with a pound of carrots each day and munching away until you have finished? It may take a while! One cup of carrot juice contains the nutrients from one pound of carrots. To this you can easily add a couple of apples, a cucumber, some celery, green peppers, and tomatoes. Your body easily assimilates these nutrients, because it does not have to undergo the lengthy digestive process of separating the juice from the pulp. Do your children eat all the vegetables they need to grow healthy bodies? If not, juicing provides them with an abundance of nutrients to create and maintain healthy cells. Drinking freshly extracted vegetable juice is the fastest way to get nutrients to your cells, thereby bringing your body to a new level of health.

When our bodies are not operating at optimum level, they need to be fed foods that are high in nutrients. Drinking fresh vegetable juice is a more natural way of obtaining nutrients than vitamins in pill form. Many people spend their money on expensive vitamin pills containing inorganic nutrients that their body discards. Our bodies are alive, however, and require live, organic nutrients, and not those that have been made from inorganic ingredients, processed, and converted to pill form. God created fresh vegetables and the juice within them. Humans cannot recreate all of the natural healthful properties found in fresh vegetables and fruits. They simply cannot be put in pill form. Drinking freshly extracted vegetable and fruit juice allows your body to absorb maximum nutrients, and is highly therapeutic for cleansing and building a healthy body.

Why the emphasis on *freshly extracted juice* rather than bottled juice? Fresh juice contains all of the enzymes, vitamins, minerals, and other nutrients that the fresh vegetables and fruits contained themselves. Most bottled, canned, or frozen juices have undergone the pasteurization process, which destroys vital nutrients, rendering most of them inorganic and unusable by our bodies. What we end up drinking with most bottled juices are empty calories (sugar water). Fresh juice contains the nutrients God created, and when you drink it, your body knows the difference! But remember that your body needs fiber, so drinking freshly extracted juice should not replace eating vegetables and fruit.

What are the best juices to drink? Vegetables tend to be loaded with vitamins, and drinking their juice gives you an amazing amount of vitality and health. Because fruit juice is high in sugar and fruit is more easily digested than vegetables, you will benefit more from drinking vegetable juice than fruit juice. When in doubt, juice your vegetables and eat your fruit. Begin drinking freshly extracted juice and watch your body come to life as it utilizes power packed nutrition to flush out old toxic waste and rebuild strong healthy cells!

If you have never juiced before and would like to begin, find a juicer with a large chute, and buy a variety of vegetables and fruit. Following are a few of my favorite recipes. Try them or create your own delicious combinations.

Carrot-Apple
2 pounds carrots
1 apple

Fresh Vegetable
2 tomatoes
1/2 pound carrots
1 celery stalk
1/2 cucumber
1/4 beet

Apple-Celery
3 apples
2 celery stalks

Veggie Combination
1/2 pound carrots
1 green pepper
1/4 beet
1/2 cucumber
1 apple

Five Fruit Juice
1 orange
2 apples
1 cup grapes
1/4 pineapple
1 pear

Carrots and Fruit
1/2 pound carrots
2 apples
1 orange

Spicy Veggies
1/2 pound carrots
1/2 cucumber
1 pear
1 clove garlic
1/2 jalapeno

Chapter 9 Study Questions

1. What is your definition of good health?

   _____

   _____

   _____

2. When and where does disease begin?

   _____

   _____

   _____

3. What are some ways you can release toxins from your body so it can build healthy new cells?

   _____

   _____

   _____

4. What is a colon cleanse, and how does it benefit your body?

   _____

   _____

   _____

5. Write Matthew 6:16.

   _____

   _____

   _____

6. Describe your current level of physical fitness.

   _____

   _____

   _____

7. List five benefits of regular exercise.

   _____

   _____

   _____

   _____

   _____

8. In order to have a healthy body, we must make exercise
   a _____.

9. Consider your lifestyle and make an exercise plan for
   yourself. Develop a plan you can stick to. Encourage
   your partner to develop his/her own plan and motivate
   one another through encouragement and mutual
   accountability.

My Exercise Plan:

_____

_____

_____

_____

_____

_____

10. Write Proverbs 27:17.

    _____

    _____

    _____

11. Why is it so important to drink an abundance of pure clean water?

    _____

    _____

    _____

12. Most people do not consume enough _____ to combat disease.

13. What are the benefits of drinking raw, freshly-extracted vegetable juice?

_____

_____

_____

14. What makes raw vegetable and fruit juice more valuable than a vitamin pill?

_____

_____

_____

15. Does bottled juice have the same benefits as raw juice? Why?

_____

_____

_____

16. What information was most interesting to you in this chapter?

_____

_____

_____

17. Are you beginning to develop a healthy plan for your life? _____

In what ways will you implement the information from Chapter 9 to build a healthier body?

_____

_____

_____

_____

_____

_____

Proverbs 16:3 says, *"Commit to the Lord whatever you do, and your plans will succeed."*

Commit your plans to the Lord now, and ask Him for the strength and will to carry them out. *"May our Lord Jesus Christ himself and God our Father, who loved us and by his grace gave us eternal encouragement and good hope, encourage your hearts and strengthen you in every good deed and word"* (2 Thessalonians 2:16).

Chapter Ten

Losing Weight, Gaining Freedom

Now the Lord is the Spirit,
and where the Spirit of the Lord is, there is freedom.
2 Corinthians 3:17

Perhaps the biggest deception that comes from the freedom of eating what we want is the lack of freedom we experience as a result of our dietary practices. While spending money on dieting and doctors, carrying around extra weight, and countless hours agonizing over the extra pounds and extra pain, we have cheated ourselves into believing we can eat what we want without paying the price. But we are paying the price! Americans spend over $40 billion per year on dieting. That is $110 million every day of the year.[1] The National Institute of Health estimates the cost to our country from obesity is over $100 billion per year.[2] This figure does not measure the emotional trauma or the time spent dealing with dieting and medical issues relating to obesity.

Why are we not succeeding in maintaining a healthy weight in America? Why is it that diet programs are not working? According to Joel Fuhrman, M.D., in *Eat to Live*, 95% of those who lose weight on a diet gain back all the weight they lost, and more, within three years.[3] The answer is that dieting is unnatural. God gave us a healthy appetite for healthy foods. He didn't require Adam and Eve to count calories, weigh-in weekly, or eat only from specific food groups on specific days. He provided them with foods that were healthy, and they ate until they were satisfied. God has given us healthy, nutritious, delicious, life-giving and disease preventing foods, but we are not eating enough of them. As Americans, typically we eat mostly refined, processed, fat-laden foods, causing us to gain weight while creating a nutritional deficiency in our bodies. We overeat, but we are malnourished. Yes, people who are overweight are frequently malnourished, and this explains their overeating and frequency of sickness and disease. We eat but are not quite satisfied, so even though our body has taken in an abundance of calories and fat, we are left desiring more. We have lost touch with our natural sense that tells us what our body needs. Consequently, we go searching for yet more food that still does not satisfy our craving for proper nutrition.

I can do everything through him who gives me strength. Philippians 4:13

Until your body has tasted good, wholesome food on a regular basis, you most likely will not recognize the desire for such foods. Instead of an apple, you may crave a cookie. Instead of a good bean chili, you may crave a hamburger. Once you begin eating the foods that God created to nourish your body, and consider what will satisfy your hunger, those fat-laden, sugar-filled foods will not hold a candle to nutrient-dense foods that were created by God.

Here is some exciting news: in order to be healthy and maintain proper body weight, you do not need to "diet" in the traditional sense of the word at all! When your lifestyle is healthy, and the foods you put into your body are healthy, you will be well on your way to your ideal weight without counting calories or carbs, weighing food, or developing a complicated weight-loss plan. The goal is to pursue health. Simply eat foods that promote health and do not contribute to disease. Eat until you are full and satisfied, and when you get hungry, eat again.

There is no need to go hungry when you are choosing natural foods such as fruits, vegetables, grains, and beans.

Maintaining a proper body weight is so much more than cosmetic. Your very health depends on it. An estimated 75% or more Americans are overweight.[4] Being overweight drastically increases your risk of death by disease. Some conditions that are caused or worsened by being overweight are hypertension, diabetes, heart disease, and cancer. Also, those who are overweight are more likely to die earlier than their thin counterparts.[5] There is, in fact, a direct correlation between obesity and a shorter life span.[6] As weight increases, mortality increases.[7] Conversely, there is also a direct link between thinness and longevity.[8] Studies show that people who are lean live longer than those who are not as lean .[9]

Real or Imaginary Freedom?

For some of you this information is not surprising, because you have battled with your weight since childhood, since your last baby was born, or since you took an office job. Whatever the cause of the initial onset of your extra weight, it produces emotional stress, and consumes precious time in worry and attempts to find a way to lose it. Are you at the end of your rope in battling your weight? Have you tried the world's ways and followed the world's thought processes of dieting and food with no lasting success? Let me ask you this. Have you tried God's way? Have you eaten the foods He has created to promote life in your body? Does this sound too radical to you? We need to discard the world's way of thinking, but it is so engrained in us that we tend to see eating healthy as radical, and even strange. But it's not! Eating healthy, healing foods brings life, health, vitality, and proper body weight. The world has complicated health and wholeness by competing for our desires. Our spirit longs for the things of Christ, while our flesh wants to taste the delicacies of this world. We need to bring our flesh in line with our Spirit and begin eating for health and wholeness rather than for earthly pleasure.

What we find in eating, and so many other areas of our life, is that when we bring our desires in line with God's, we discover great freedom! So many times we have thought we were free, only to realize we were in bondage. We may have been free to follow our own desires, but that does not give us the freedom God desires for us. The bondage that comes from following our own desires soon overtakes us. We think we have the freedom to eat whatever we like—whatever tastes good, and whatever the world says is good, without weighing the consequences. But God says there are consequences for our actions. *Whatever we sow, we will reap* (Galatians 6:7). Are you sowing for sickness or health? Are you sowing for longevity or a short life? Which seeds are *you* planting?

When you sow the seeds of good health, you are also sowing seeds for a healthy body weight. There is great freedom when you

Your body is the baggage you must carry through life. The more excess the baggage, the shorter the trip.
Arnold H. Glasgow

do not have to worry about, or even consider your weight! Can you imagine that? Have you lived so long being conscious of your weight and what you should eat, that you cannot imagine the true freedom that comes from choosing foods that God has designed for your body? How often do you feel guilty when you eat? Can you picture eating until you are full every time you are hungry with *no guilt* and no concern over sickness and disease? That is what I call freedom! It's the type of freedom God offers you—not just the ability to choose, but the ability to choose well and reap the rewards.

You can lose weight and maintain a healthy weight without following the world's ways of dieting. You will be increasing the vitamins, minerals and other nutrients your body receives, while gaining improved digestion. You will most likely begin to lose weight without the hassles previously experienced from traditional diets. In fact, if you have never been able to lose weight on a diet, and keep it off, you are likely to have great success with this plan. In addition, you will feel so much better physically and emotionally, sleep better, have more energy, and become healthier overall. You will have no need to fear sickness and disease, and you will be eating until you are satisfied each and every time you are hungry, with *no guilt!*

Losing Weight the Healthy Way

Prepare yourself—losing weight on this plan can be so much fun, you might get excited! First, I will lay out some general guidelines to follow, and then give you some specific suggestions for carrying them through. In order to lose weight and become healthy, you must begin eating foods that are beneficial to your body. Eat foods that are rich in fiber and nutrients— fruits, vegetables, beans, and whole grains. These foods will fill you up and satisfy you, unlike refined or fat-laden foods. A 1 1/2- ounce serving of potato chips, for example, contains the same amount of calories as a baked potato. The potato would satisfy your appetite, but you would still be hungry after eating the potato chips. Fat stimulates your appetite—the more you eat, the more you want. When you eat meat, dairy, and oil, you eat more calories than you need before you are full. But when you eat unrefined foods high in nutrients and fiber, you fill up quickly and are satisfied without eating too many calories or too much fat. Eating a diet full of high-fiber foods will help you feel full quicker and stay full longer, and it offers a host of other health benefits, including protection against cancer, heart disease, constipation, hemorrhoids, diabetes, varicose veins, and hormonal imbalances.[10]

> Then Jesus declared, "I am the bread of life. He who comes to me will never go hungry, and he who believes in me will never be thirsty.
> John 6:35

If you have health issues that should be monitored by your doctor, or you are on medication, consult your doctor before beginning any weight loss program. He may need to monitor you to adjust your medication as you lose weight and gain wellness.

Some general guidelines for losing weight while gaining a healthy body include limiting or omitting meat, dairy, refined foods, and refined oils. If you want to see results quickly, I recommend entirely omitting the above foods. *Eat freely of unrefined plant foods.* Eat when you are hungry, and eat until you are full. Genesis 2:16 says, *"And the Lord God commanded man, saying, 'of every tree of the garden you may freely eat;'"* (NKJV). This does not mean we can be gluttonous, but we can satisfy our natural God-given hunger. When you want to eat, be sure you are actually hungry. We often eat for other reasons, such as boredom, comfort, anxiety, loneliness, depression, anger, enjoyment, procrastination and celebration.[11]

Following are some tips for a successful weight-loss plan:

◆ Eat raw vegetables in *unlimited* quantities… the more the better. *Don't limit* the amount of salad you eat at lunch or dinner. Make sure you choose a dressing that is not high in fat.

◆ Be creative with the vegetables on your salad. Include a variety of vegetables, even if they are new to you. Here are some to get you started: red, green, yellow, or purple bell peppers, banana peppers, green peas, snow peas, sugar snap peas, alfalfa sprouts, bean sprouts, broccoli sprouts, carrots, tomatoes, cucumbers, broccoli, cauliflower, celery, and corn. Don't forget to try different varieties of lettuce, such as Romaine, green leaf, red leaf, Boston, and Bibb.

- Eat your salad first at each meal.
- Eat a *large* amount of lightly steamed green veggies, such as spinach, kale, turnip greens, etc.
- Eat a lot of other steamed veggies, such as broccoli, cauliflower, cabbage, zucchini, eggplant, peppers, string beans, peas, and asparagus. *Don't limit your portions.* Eat until you are satisfied.
- Eat as many beans and legumes as you desire. They are loaded with fiber, protein, and other valuable nutrients, and they help you feel full. Eat at least one serving of beans a day.
- Eat at least four servings of fresh fruit a day. Try different varieties, such as apples, oranges, clementines, tangerines, mangoes, papayas, cantaloupe, pineapple, pears, peaches, plums, cherries, grapes, raspberries, strawberries, blackberries, blueberries, grapefruits, and kiwis.
- Drink plenty of water in between meals, and drink freshly extracted vegetable juices if desired. Most beverages contain empty calories that cause weight gain or even chemicals that can harm your body. When choosing beverages, make sure they are beneficial to your body. Water, freshly extracted vegetable juice, and herbal teas are all good choices.
- Avoid temptation by removing foods you will not be eating from your house. Remember, if you don't need to eat refined foods, dairy products, meat, or sugary desserts, neither do your children. Remove these harmful foods from your house and fill it with healthy foods. Your children may need to eat more fat and calories than you if you are focusing on weight loss, so be sure to have plenty of nuts, nut butters, avocados, starchy vegetables, and grains available for them.
- Oils are made of 100% fat. Any fat can be deposited unchanged in your body within minutes.[12] Avoid processed oils and foods cooked in oil.

◆ Eat nuts, flax seed, and other seeds in limited quantities to obtain your essential fatty acids. If you cannot eat nuts or seeds, but can eat the oil from them, take 1-2 tablespoons of flax oil or Udo's oil a day.

◆ Always have healthy foods on-hand, prepared, and ready to eat.

◆ Social events can be difficult experiences for someone trying to obtain health or lose weight. Here are some tips:

1. Eat a healthy meal or snack before you leave your house.
2. If you are attending an event where you bring food to share, bring a healthy, filling food that you can eat.
3. Scope out the food table, and decide what you can eat.
4. Always carry a snack with you—fresh fruit, nuts, a slice of whole grain bread, etc.
5. Remember your goals and ask yourself if the food you are eating will help you reach them.

◆ Be sure to have at least one good friend who has an understanding of what you are doing, and is willing to support you. Having someone to hold you accountable and discuss your success is motivating.

If you are eating enough of the right kinds of foods, there will be no room left in your diet for harmful foods. You will feel full and satisfied by eating foods that are loaded with nutrients and fiber, the way God created them.

Pay close attention to when and why you eat. Eat three meals a day, and snack on fresh fruits or vegetables when you are hungry. Breakfast can consist of fresh fruit or a smoothie if you are the type of person who is not hungry in the morning. If you are hungry at night after dinner, eat fresh fruit. Recognize the difference between true hunger and withdrawal symptoms from food.

Some symptoms of withdrawal from meat, sugar, refined foods, and caffeine can include feeling shaky, lightheaded, or having a headache. After eating nutrient-dense foods and eliminating unhealthy foods, you will be surprised at how long you can go without eating, and without the uncomfortable symptoms that may have been a part of your everyday life.

My doctor told me to stop having intimate dinners for four. Unless there are three other people.
Orson Wells

The Lord has blessed us with so many delicious foods for our nourishment and enjoyment. I trust you will never look at the fresh produce section of the grocery store the same way again!

May the Lord's hand be upon you as you make choices for health, not sickness, and for life, not death. May He become your strength to enable you to fulfill His purposes for your life. May you enjoy all good things He has created for you, and may you honor His name by being obedient to the call He has placed on your life

Praise the Lord, O my soul;
all my inmost being, praise his holy name.
Praise the Lord, O my soul,
and forget not all his benefits—
who forgives all your sins
and heals all your diseases,
who redeems your life from the pit
and crowns you with love and compassion,
who satisfies your desires with good things
so that your youth is renewed like the eagle's.
Psalm 103:1-5

Losing Weight, Feeling Great

Unlimited Raw Vegetables

Salad First at Each Meal

Steamed Veggies in Abundance

Beans and Legumes—As Many as You Like

Fresh Fruit—At Least Four Servings a Day

Water and Herbal Teas—Enjoy Freely

Avoid refined foods, meat, dairy products, processed oils, and fried foods.

Chapter 10 Study Questions

1. Have you ever been on a diet? Describe your experience with maintaining a healthy body weight.

   _____

   _____

   _____

   _____

   _____

2. Describe some problems associated with dieting.

   _____

   _____

   _____

   _____

   _____

3. What percentage of Americans are overweight?

   _____

4. _____% of those who lose weight on a diet gain back all of the weight they lost and more within three years.

5. List four health conditions that are caused or worsened by being overweight.

   _____

   _____

   _____

   _____

6. If you are overweight, what are some of the negative aspects you experience, both in health and other areas?

   _____

   _____

   _____

7. What are the general principles of health and weight loss?

   _____

   _____

   _____

8. List some reasons we eat other than for hunger.

   _____

   _____

   _____

Do you eat for any of these reasons? If so, which ones?

_____

_____

_____

9. What are some symptoms of food withdrawal from meat, sugar, refined foods, and caffeine?

   _____

   _____

   _____

10. Summarize each main point of the "tips for a successful weight-loss program."

    _____

    _____

    _____

    _____

    _____

    _____

    _____

11. Describe the freedom you would experience if you could maintain a healthy body and healthy body weight without dieting or feeling hungry and deprived.

_____

_____

_____

12. If you are overweight, even by a few pounds, the first thing you can do to achieve a healthy body is to lose the extra weight by eating healthful foods, and keep it off.

    Create a personal plan for yourself and make a commitment to stick to it. This is an exciting day! The freedom you will discover from eating the foods God created for you will far outweigh your temporary cravings for foods that have caused so many problems in your body.

    Give thanks to the Lord, for he is good;
    his love endures forever.
    1 Chronicles 16:9

My personal plan for losing weight while gaining health:

_____

_____

_____

_____

_____

_____

_____

_____

_____

_____

_____

_____

_____

_____

_____

_____

_____

_____

_____

_____

_____

Then Jesus declared, "I am the bread of life. He who comes to me will never go hungry, and he who believes in me will never be thirsty."

John 6:35

Chapter Eleven

Your Entrée into Bountiful Health

*Let us not become weary in doing good, for at the proper time
we will reap a harvest if we do not give up.*
Galatians 6:9

With all of this newfound knowledge, you might be eager to get rid of those harmful foods that cause sickness and disease, and begin eating and enjoying life-giving foods. It's time to look in your refrigerator, pantry, and cupboards and begin to make exchanges. Getting rid of those unhealthy foods in your home is the first step to a new and healthy you! Start reading labels and toss those foods that are harmful to your body or are mere empty calories. Replace them with life-giving foods, such as fruits, vegetables, whole grains, beans, and nuts.

To gain health or maintain a healthy body, you need to eat foods that are high in nutrients in proportion to calories. For example, fruits and vegetables are high in nutrients and fiber, but low in calories. Meat is low in nutrients, contains no fiber, and is high in calories. Foods containing refined flour and sugar are low in nutrients and fiber, but relatively high in calories. Which foods will you benefit from? Your body will become healthy only when it receives the nutrients it requires from the foods you eat. It is very important to consider the foods you put in your mouth and eat not only for taste, but for nutrition.

Raw vegetables and fruits offer more protection against cancer than any other foods,[1] and eating large amounts of unrefined plant foods offers the greatest protection against disease. Remember, you don't have to limit the amount of food you eat when you are eating unrefined plant foods, because they are so beneficial to your body. Your body actually requires nutrients from these foods to grow healthy cells, and healthy cells are required to maintain a healthy body.

> *Good food ends with good talk.*
> *Geoffrey Neighor*

Eat as many raw vegetables and as many steamed vegetables a day as you can. Eat at least four pieces of fresh fruit a day. Feast on as many cooked beans and legumes as you would like—make sure you eat some every day. In addition to these foods, whole grains are wonderful side dishes that add fiber to your meal and help you feel full. With meals of raw and steamed vegetables, beans, and whole grains, you will get an abundance of nutrients. These foods are amazingly tasty and satisfying, and you will feel full before you have the opportunity to eat a dangerous amount of fat or an excessive amount of calories. Cravings begin to disappear when you fill your body with natural unprocessed foods, and you will feel satisfied after you have eaten.

Make sure you eat when you are hungry, and that you keep plenty of fresh live fruits and vegetables on hand for snacking and mealtime. Remember, canned, cooked, fortified boxed foods, and vitamin pills cannot take the place of eating fresh fruits and vegetables. Your body knows the difference. If you have never eaten healthy foods for a long enough period of time to see the benefits, you will be amazed at the way you feel, and how your body seems to work out its problems and heal its diseases naturally!

Here are some varieties of whole natural foods that you can begin to add to your diet:

Vegetables

Artichoke
Asparagus
Avocado
Beans
Broccoli
Cauliflower
Cabbage
Celery
Carrots
Cucumbers
Red pepper
Green pepper
Yellow pepper
Banana pepper
Jalapeno pepper
Poblano pepper
Arugula
Green leaf lettuce
Red leaf lettuce
Romaine lettuce
Watercress
Kohlrabi
Corn
Mustard greens
Kale
Okra
Chives
Garlic
Leeks
Onions
Shallots
Beets
Parsnips
Radishes
Turnips
Spinach
Acorn squash
Butternut squash
Spaghetti squash
Yellow squash
Zucchini squash
Potatoes
Sweet potatoes

Fruits

Apples
Apricots
Cherries
Pears
Plums
Peaches
Nectarines
Kiwis
Watermelon
Cantaloupe
Honeydew
Grapes
Figs
Pomegranates
Dates
Grapefruits
Oranges
Lemons
Limes
Clementines
Tangelos
Bananas
Coconuts
Mangos
Pineapples
Strawberries
Blackberries
Raspberries
Bearberries
Blueberries
Cranberries
Huckleberries
Currants
Elderberries
Gooseberries

Grains

Wheat
Barley
Oats
Rye
Triticale
Buckwheat
Spelt
Rice
Maize
Millet
Amaranth
Quinoa

Nuts

Almonds
Walnuts
Pecans
Pistachios
Chestnuts
Macadamias
Brazils
Cashews
Hazelnuts
Pine nuts

Seeds

Pumpkin
Sesame
Sunflower
Flax

Beans

Adzuki beans
Pink beans
Small red beans
Dark red
  kidney beans
Light red
  kidney beans
Black beans
Navy beans
Baby lima beans
Black-eyed peas
Pinto beans

Great Northern
  beans
Garbanzo beans
  (chick peas)
Lentils
Dry peas

Herbs

Balm
Basil
Chervil
Chives
Cilantro
Coriander

Dill
Fennel
Lavender
Lemongrass
Marjoram
Mint
Mustard
Oregano
Parsley
Rosemary
Sage
Savory
Tarragon
Thyme

She is like the merchant ships, bringing her food from afar.
She gets up while it is still dark;
she provides food for her family
and portions for her servant girls.
Proverbs 31:14-15

Three-Day Meal Plan

Following is a sample three-day meal plan so you can easily begin to implement this life-giving, life-changing lifestyle.

Day 1
Breakfast: Apple Cinnamon Pancakes
Ingredients:

3 eggs
2 c. rice milk
1 c. applesauce
2 Tbsp. oil
3 1/4 cup whole wheat
  bread flour

2 1/3 Tbsp. baking powder
1 1/2 tsp. salt
1 tsp. cinnamon

Directions:

Beat eggs. Mix in milk, applesauce and oil. Stir in flour, baking powder, salt, and cinnamon. Bake on hot griddle. Serve with pure maple syrup.

Lunch: Raspberry Spinach Salad and Roasted Vegetables
Raspberry Salad:
Ingredients:

4 cups spinach leaves,
  washed and dried
1/4 red onion, thinly sliced
1/4 c. roasted sunflower
  seeds
2 Tbsp. raspberry jam
1 1/2 Tbsp. olive oil

2 Tbsp. red wine vinegar
1/4 tsp. onion powder
1/4 tsp. garlic powder
1/4 tsp. paprika
salt and pepper, to taste

Directions:

Layer spinach, onion, and sunflower seeds in a bowl. In separate bowl, combine last eight ingredients and mix well. Pour over spinach salad just before serving.

Roasted Vegetables:
Ingredients:

1 head cauliflower, cut in florets

6 carrots, quartered and cut in 2 inch pieces

2 zucchini, halved a cut in 1/2 inch slices

2 onions, sliced

1 green bell pepper, sliced

4 garlic cloves, halved

1/4 tsp. marjoram

1/4 tsp. basil

1/4 tsp, thyme

2 Tbsp. olive oil

salt and pepper, to taste

Directions:

Preheat oven to 450°. Place first six ingredients in a large baking dish. In separate bowl, mix remaining ingredients. Pour over vegetables. Bake uncovered at 450° for 25 minutes, or until vegetables are crisp-tender.

Dinner: Simply Delicious Vegetable Pot Pie

Ingredients:

1 1/2 c. frozen peas

2 c. fresh carrots, chopped

1 1/2 c. frozen corn

1 onion, chopped

2 celery stalks, chopped

2 Tbsp. olive oil

5 c. vegetable broth

2 Tbsp. corn starch

2 1/2 c. whole wheat bread flour

2 c. rice milk

2/3 c. oil

1 Tbsp. baking powder

1/2 tsp salt

Directions:

Preheat oven to 450°. Place peas and carrots in a saucepan. Cover with water and bring to a boil. Lower heat and simmer until vegetables are almost soft. Add corn. Heat until corn is thawed. Drain. Meanwhile, sauté onion and celery in oil. Sprinkle with salt. Mix 1 1/2 cups broth with cornstarch. Pour in pan with onions and celery. Heat to boiling, stirring constantly. Add the peas, carrots, and corn mixture, and remaining broth. Bring to a boil. Pour in a 9x13 inch baking dish.

In separate bowl, mix remaining ingredients. Pour over hot vegetable mixture. Bake at 450° for 20 minutes or until bubbly and bread topping browns. Delicious!

Day 2
Breakfast: Toasted Almond Granola
Ingredients:

1/3 c. pure maple syrup	1/2 c. oat bran
1/4 c. oil	1/4 tsp. sea salt
1 tsp. almond extract	1/4 c. chopped dates
4 c. rolled oats	1/2 c. chopped almonds
1/2 c. wheat bran	

Directions:
Preheat oven to 350°. Spray two large pans with cooking spray. Mix oil, syrup, and almond extract in a small bowl. Mix oats, wheat germ, oat bran, and salt in a large bowl. Put syrup mixture on oat combination and mix well. Spread mixture in pans. Bake 15 minutes, stirring every 5 minutes. Add almonds and dates. Bake 5 more minutes. Cool. Serve in a bowl with rice milk.

Lunch: Potato Leek Soup with Green Leaf Salad and Fruit Salad
Potato Leek Soup:
Ingredients:

2 Tbsp. olive oil	3 pounds potatoes, peeled and diced
1 onion, chopped	
3 leeks, chopped (white part only)	1 1/2 tsp. rosemary
	1 1/2 tsp. Italian seasoning
2 garlic cloves, chopped	vegetable broth to cover

Directions:
Sauté onion, leeks, and garlic in olive oil. Add remaining ingredients, and cook till tender. Mash potatoes to desired consistency. Serve.

Fruit Salad:
Ingredients:

3 apples, diced

2 peaches, sliced

3 bananas, sliced

1 c. grapes, halved

1 kiwi, sliced

1/4 c. maple syrup

Directions:

Combine ingredients and mix well.

Dinner: Mexican Salad with Black Beans and Guacamole
Mexican Salad:
Ingredients:

5 c. green leaf or Romaine
lettuce, chopped

1 red bell pepper, chopped

1/2 green bell pepper,
chopped

15oz. canned kidney beans,
rinsed and drained

1 c. frozen corn, thawed

1/2 c. black olives, sliced

1/2 c. onions, chopped

1 tomato, diced

crushed tortilla chips

Directions:

Layer ingredients in order. Top with your favorite dressing.

Black Beans:
Ingredients:

30 oz. canned black beans,
rinsed and drained

3 garlic cloves, crushed

2 Tbsp. fresh cilantro,
chopped

1/4 c. onion, chopped

1 tsp. chili powder

1/2 tsp. cumin

enough water for creamy
consistency

juice of 1 lime

Directions:

Combine all ingredients except limejuice in a saucepan on medium heat. Bring to a boil. Turn heat to low, and simmer for 15 minutes. Add limejuice. Mash beans slightly with potato masher.

Guacamole:
Ingredients:
   2 avocados, mashed
   1/4 tsp. onion powder
   1/4 tsp. garlic powder
   juice of 1 lime
   salt, to taste

Directions:
Combine all ingredients in a bowl or food processor until creamy.

Presentation of the meal:
Place a generous helping of Mexican Salad on a dinner plate. Put a serving of black beans and a large spoonful of guacamole beside the salad. Top beans with a spoonful of fresh salsa. Delicious!

Day 3
Breakfast: Apple Crisp Porridge

Ingredients:

2 tart apples, diced	1/4 tsp. sea salt
1/4 cup Sucanat, or	2 c. water
turbinado, or brown sugar	2 c. oats
1/2 tsp. cinnamon	1/8 c. ground flax seeds
1/4 tsp. nutmeg	2 c. rice milk

Directions:
Combine first six ingredients in a saucepan and bring to a boil. Reduce heat and simmer for 5 minutes. Add remaining ingredients and bring to a boil. Mix well and serve. Yum!

Lunch: Hummus Pita with Green Leaf Salad
Hummus:
Ingredients:

30 oz. canned chick peas,
  rinsed and drained
2 garlic cloves
juice of 1 lemon
2 Tbsp. olive oil

pepper, to taste
water, enough for creamy
  consistency
pita bread

Directions:
Blend all ingredients except bread in food processor until smooth. Spread a generous portion of hummus in pita and top with desired ingredients. Some suggestions for toppings are fresh vegetables such as cucumbers, carrots, tomatoes, onions, and peppers (chopped or sliced), sautéed onions and peppers, balsamic vinegar, and Greek or Italian dressing.

Dinner: Bean and Lentil Soup with Green Leaf Salad
and Whole Wheat Bread
Bean and Lentil Soup:
Ingredients:

2 Tbsp. olive oil
4 carrots, chopped
2 celery stalks, sliced
1 onion, chopped
2 garlic cloves, minced
54 oz. vegetable broth
15 oz. canned, diced tomatoes
1 c. dried lentils

1/2 c. barley, uncooked
1 c. frozen corn
1 tsp. thyme
1/2 tsp. rosemary
1/2 tsp. oregano
15 oz. black-eyed peas
hot sauce, to taste

Directions:
Sauté first five ingredients in large pan. Add remaining ingredients, except black-eyed peas. Bring to a boil. Reduce heat. Simmer until lentils and barley are tender. Add black-eyed peas. Simmer 5 more minutes.

Chapter 11 Study Questions

1. In order to maintain a healthy body, what foods should you eat in abundance?

   _____

   _____

   _____

2. What foods should you limit or omit?

   _____

   _____

   _____

3. This week, spend some time experimenting with new foods and new recipes.

4. Keep a record of the new foods you and your family particularly like. Be sure to add these into next week's menu.

   _____

   _____

   _____

Finally, brothers, whatever is true, whatever is noble, whatever is right, whatever is pure, whatever is lovely, whatever is admirable—if anything is excellent or praiseworthy—think about such things.
Philippians 4:8

Chapter Twelve

Running a Victorious Race: Seasoned With Perseverance, Topped Off With Grace

Do you not know that in a race all the runners run,
but only one gets the prize?
Run in such a way as to get the prize.
1 Corinthians 9:24

How do you go about creating a plan for eating life-giving foods that will work for you? First and foremost, it must be healthy. Second, it must be practical. I don't believe that counting calories, counting carbs, going hungry, or weighing yourself daily are going to work long-term. These are not practical ways to lose weight or to obtain a healthy body. Weighing daily puts undue pressure on you, causing stress and lack of joy. "Diet" should not be thought of as a short-term word, used only for weight loss, but a long-term lifestyle that leads to a healthy, vibrant body. As you work toward your goal of being healthy, you will achieve proper body weight. I ask you now to set aside everything this world has taught you about weight loss and maintenance, and focus on health instead.

Begin Anew

When deciding to choose healthy, whole foods rather than refined substances, you must first decide how radical you will be. Will you make small changes and gradually work toward a healthy lifestyle, or will you make the change all at once, removing the harmful foods and substituting healthful ones? Research has shown that it is easier to make comprehensive changes in eating habits than it is to make moderate ones.[1] When you make moderate changes in your diet, for example, reducing the amount of meat you eat each day, or adding one piece of fruit and one extra serving of vegetables, it appears to be a smart move, and it is. Changes like this, however, are not significant enough for your body to notice much difference. Although you are taking steps toward health, it will be a long and drawn out process, and if you don't see early results, you will probably question why you are making the effort to begin with! It is very likely that when making only moderate changes to your diet, you will not feel significantly better, and will have a difficult time sticking to it. You may still have trouble with excess weight, and not see significant changes in blood pressure, cholesterol, skin condition, or any other issues you may be dealing with.

Every day they continued to meet together in the temple courts. They broke bread in their homes and ate together with glad and sincere hearts.
Acts 27:35

If you omit some of your favorite foods, and don't see significant results, you won't have much motivation to go on! If you continue eating the foods you crave, however, even in smaller servings, you will still maintain a taste for them and the desire to eat them at every opportunity. You might be addicted to sugar, the taste of meat, and to comfort foods that are traditions in your life. The idea of simply reducing the quantity of these foods, however, can leave you feeling uncomfortable and deprived.

Contrast the above attempt at moderation with a person who totally reprograms the way she views food. By making comprehensive changes in her diet, she sees tremendous changes in her body and the way she feels! Her excess weight seems to disappear day by day, the aches and pains she has always lived with diminish and disappear, her skin becomes vibrant, and she feels great! No one has to tell her that what she is doing is good for her: she knows it by the way her body looks and feels! Do you think this person is likely to feel deprived because she has chosen new and more valuable foods for her body? No way! The effort is worth the results she is achieving! In fact, she may become indignant that she has struggled with health issues her whole life, only to find out that the vast majority of her struggles were caused by the very foods she was eating! A person with this experience will not soon return to her old ways of eating. She will have far too much at stake with both truth and success under her belt.

I challenge you to use the following standard when choosing food: does this particular food bring life, or does it bring death? In other words, does it provide proper building blocks for my cells, or does it cause stress to my body, eventually leading to disease? Rather than simply omitting some of your favorite foods, re-evaluate all the foods you eat. Do they bring life, or do they bring death? What can you eat in place of the bad foods that will satisfy your taste buds and your desire for good food? Consider what each food is doing for your body as you are eating it. Pray that God will bless each bite of the healthy food and use it to nourish your body to the fullest. Now, can you say the same prayer over food that you know is damaging to your body, the Temple of the Holy Spirit? You can't hide from God. Make this the greatest adventure of your life! With a little knowledge under your belt, you can achieve your goals and more without counting calories, weighing daily, or feeling hungry and deprived.

Me, My Family, or Both?

You may be thinking that changing the way you eat isn't easy when you are feeding your husband and children different foods, and you are right! My motto is, "If it's good for me, it's good for them!" Most typical diets are not good for us, let alone our children. But we are now focusing on health and life, which is good

Always laugh when you can. It is cheap medicine.
Lord Byron

for all of us! As a wife and mother, I do most of the meal planning, shopping, and meal and snack preparation for my family. Therefore the responsibility falls primarily on me as to whether or not my husband and children eat healthy foods. This is pivotal, because we are obligated to raise our children with the fear and admonition of the Lord. How can we do this while we pile junk food into their bodies just as the world does? They get just as sick, are more overweight than ever, and will end up diseased as adults if they maintain the standard American diet. So why would we choose to eat healthy, life giving foods, but feed our husband and children substances that were never intended to be put into their bodies? We are in a position to teach and train our children in the things of life and godliness. Let's not forsake the training of proper nutrition, which brings healing to the body.

Now, let's discuss how you can actually feed your family foods that will bring life and healing.

1. First you need to know what these foods are. You are getting an excellent start by reading this book, but please don't stop there! Locate and read some of the books on my recommended reading list. This will further your knowledge and your motivation to continue.

2. Next, see if your husband is willing to come on board. Narrow down your "information darts" to only a few, and see if he is willing to read selected informational sections of this book. Discuss the changes you would like to make regarding food, and exactly why you would like to make them. Go to him with a plan so your ideas do not seem ambiguous or short-lived. You may have to prove to him you are serious by sticking with your plan for more than two weeks! It always helps to also have a friend who can support you with encouragement and ideas.

3. Third, call your children together and talk with them about some menu changes you will be making as a family and why. Make it sound exciting, and have some fun food events planned to make this a great experience for them!

4. Begin taking brief moments to share with your children how certain foods can bring healing or harm to their bodies. Share scriptures you read in this book and others that are pertinent to helping your family make good choices. Pray with them. Lay out the list of foods that are not going to be eaten for a while (or not at all), and from a list of fun new foods, ask which ones they want to try. This can be a great, life-changing, good-habit forming time in your children's lives.

5. Grow a garden if you have any space at all to do so. This can be so much fun for both you and the children, not to mention great exercise. Children tend to eat the foods they grow, and often prefer to stand in the garden and eat them raw. One year my family had the mysterious problem of our sugar snap peas disappearing. Every day when I went out to check the garden, there were plenty of small, unripe pods, but no large ones. They never seemed to grow! At least that is what I thought until I found my four year old daughter standing amongst the plants, eating away. She was continuously eating them all before we even had a chance to harvest. This has also happened with cherry tomatoes, and even parsley and chives (yuk!). What a way for our kids to eat their vegetables—just as God created them!

6. Encourage your children to help you in the kitchen. Children love to cook. They should be a part of meal preparation because they consume the food! In this day and age, we tend to raise our children to be consumers but not producers. Let your children feel like they are really a part of the family by helping. Even a three year old can be a big help in small ways. Depending on their

age, children are especially good at tearing up lettuce for a salad, measuring and pouring ingredients into a bowl, mixing, putting away silverware from the dishwasher, setting the table, getting out ingredients, cooking simple foods (pancakes, rice, barley, beans, teas, oatmeal, etc.), and they can be great with kitchen cleanup! Working with your children in the kitchen gives them the effectual knowledge that they are a part of your working family, and it is a great time to share information about what foods you are preparing and why. It also gives you a regular time to discuss what's on their minds, sing songs together, or just plain have fun!

After taking all the fun and motivational steps to encourage your children to eat healthy foods, you need your children to actually eat the foods! The above ideas will help set a positive tone for trying new foods and establishing new eating patterns. But after all of this positive reinforcement, what do you do when you sit down at the table and you have a child who refuses to eat what you have prepared on a regular basis? First, determine if you have actually created a positive atmosphere for eating. Second, assess what you are cooking, and decide if you can reasonably expect your kids to eat it. Even my kids would practically gag if I placed an eggplant soufflé in front of them! Most recipes in this book are extremely family friendly. It will take a while, however, for your family's taste buds to change if they are used to dining on meals of meat and refined foods. This is one reason why a comprehensive change is easier to make than a small to moderate one.

Your children need to understand that as their parents, you know what is best for them. Then help them understand why certain foods are good for their bodies, and how you are honoring God when you make good food choices. Gently let them know that God created these foods, and we are going to thankfully eat them. If you have a child who pushes their plate away at the table or refuses to eat what you have prepared, you not only have a picky eater, but you are also dealing with disobedience and ungratefulness, both of which should be addressed.

Many parents ask me how I have managed to get my kids to eat the foods they do. After following the above steps for setting the stage for success, I simply require them to eat what they are served at the table. Each child is obviously different. If you tell one child he will not eat for the rest of the night if he leaves the table, he will willingly scarf down his food. For another child, this is not a huge consequence. Some children are not big eaters and do not mind missing a meal. Remember to bring your kids to the dinner table hungry. Offering them a snack right before dinner when preparing a food that is not their favorite will cause distress at the dinner table! What we want is a peaceful meal where our bodies are nourished and we can share pleasant conversation. After some training, I can assure you this is possible. Have you trained your children to like unhealthy foods? Have you often fed them separate foods when you created something healthy for yourself? Have they frequently dined on hot dogs, fish sticks, French fries, Spaghettios, canned green beans, pizza, and the like? If so, you will need to be steady and persistent in changing their diets to health and life-giving foods!

May your walls know joy; May every room hold laughter and every window open to great possibility.
Maryanne Radmacher-Hershey

Choosing meals and snacks your family is more likely to enjoy will give you a good start, but if mealtime is still more like a battle than a walk in the park, keep in mind that you are training your children in more than healthy eating. You are training them to have respect for the person who prepared the meal, as well as those sitting at the table with them. You are also training them in thankfulness—that God has provided for their needs, and in obedience—that they obey fully even when it is not pleasant for them.

When parents ask me how I trained my children to eat lentil stew, vegetable stir fry, black bean burritos, etc., I tell them this: when my children come to the table, they are not to complain about what they are served. Any complaint will be met with a warning. If that same child complains again, they leave the table for the remainder of the night. For my children, this is a severe consequence! If your children don't mind going hungry, then you will need to use a different strategy. My children are expected to eat a reasonable amount of what they are served without whining or complaining. You will not hear me tell them to eat one bite or three bites. When I give instructions in bites, it is ten or more! I do not believe children are trained in obedience when we negotiate parameters with them. In our home, at the meal table, we set the parameters for them. When our children do not obey, there are consequences. The consequence for disobedience must be applied swiftly and calmly, and the child must know that it will be applied, even when inconvenient for the parent. They will thank you for this in the future. My kids already do! My eight and ten year old children easily detect when a child is not required to obey at home. They actually let me know that such children are not pleasant to be around!

Now for some encouragement—it took my children only about three weeks to begin really enjoying the new and unusual foods they are now eating. I remember when we first began eating healthy foods on a regular basis. My daughter, who was five

Let us not become weary in doing good, for at the proper time we will reap a harvest if we do not give up.
Galatians 6:9

at the time, asked what was for dinner one night, and I told her "lentil stew." She said, "Mmmm. Lentil stew, my favorite!" and I knew we had victory. I often serve homemade whole wheat bread with a meal, and many times they must eat what is on their plates before they may have bread. This can be a good motivator using any healthy food your children like. We frequently eat salad for lunch with whole wheat bread on the side. My children love it, and are even more grateful when we add fun toppings like mandarin oranges, chopped olives, corn, or kidney beans. I am told on a regular basis that my children are a joy to feed. It blesses me to hear these reports, and I let my children know!

Breakfast, lunch, and snack times are a great time for memorizing scriptures in thankfulness, obedience, and other topics as a family. Review them in a positive light at dinner. Keep a notebook of all memorized scripture, and review it periodically. You and your children will stand in awe of God and His goodness the more you focus on Him! We spend a lot of time eating in our lifetime! When combined with learning, speaking, and reciting scripture, mealtimes then become a time to not only satisfy our physical hunger, but our spiritual hunger as well.

The amazing thing is that when our family made this transition, it was fun. It was an adventure! My husband would call home from work and jokingly ask if we were having "vegetable casserole or vegetable pizza" for dinner, and I would say, "Oh, no, tonight it is vegetable pie!" He told me that as long as it tasted good and was filling, he would gladly eat what I prepared. Sometimes meals were a struggle (and still can be, on occasion), but we follow through with our convictions. Gladly accepting mealtime as yet another training ground for our children, and not simply a time for us to give in to their desires, will benefit all of us greatly, both now and in the future.

A Few More Tips...

◆ Personal motivation and knowledge will carry you a long way in making dietary and lifestyle changes. Ask yourself, "What is my primary motivation?"

◆ Once your new eating practices become habits, and you see the benefits, maintaining a healthy lifestyle can be a real joy, and much easier than you thought it would be.

◆ Your taste buds and desire for food will change with knowledge and dietary changes. Good foods will become appealing, and bad foods will not seem like food at all. Remember to ask, "Does this food bring life (health) or death (sickness)?"

◆ A commitment for a particular time period with specific guidelines can help you get through the initial stage when you crave the old foods.

◆ Find someone who has already made the change or is committed to making it, and encourage one another daily. Share Scripture and recipes. If you need more support than this, take a vegetarian cooking class or find a person who is further along on this journey who can mentor you.

◆ You do not need to go hungry and deprive yourself! There is such a large variety of foods to choose from. Make it an adventure and enjoy it! Try new foods and recipes, and eat when you are hungry.

◆ Make mealtime an event to enjoy.

◆ Stay focused on your goal of becoming healthy. It is a lifestyle. Don't worry if you temporarily deviate from your plan. Just get back on track and keep going.

◆ Keep it simple. A lifestyle of health may take some time to implement, but eating healthy foods is not difficult or complicated. It is natural.

Summing it All Up

When you choose the road to health rather than sickness and disease, you will be on the path less traveled. People around you will see your food choices and healthy lifestyle as "different." They may notice your new and lower weight, your increased energy level, fresh outlook on life, and abounding vitality. You might assume these people will be happy for you, and some will be. But sadly, many will pass judgment and tell you that you are deprived, and that certainly your children must be…since they are not able to "enjoy" junk foods like other children do! I simply answer and say, "Deprived, no way. Free? Yes!" Continue on in the freedom of Christ, and your life will speak clearly to those around you.

Finishing the Race

This has been an exciting journey, hasn't it? From taking a look at your current physical condition to considering what Scripture says, from learning what will bring your body vibrant health to practically applying this information, you have taken the time to learn the secrets of giving your body life, health, and healing. What better gift can you give yourself and your loved ones than the gift of full, vibrant, and complete health? No longer do you have to fear disease or battle weight, no longer do you have to suffer from the pain and inconvenience of physical issues in your body. You have reason to hope in God and in His Word, that He did create a marvelous and miraculous body, ready to heal itself when given the proper tools.

I hope you are encouraged with the results you are already achieving, that you have found support to help you carry on, and that these new habits will form a beautifully healthy and fulfilling lifestyle. May the Lord grant you peace and wisdom, health and life as you continue on your journey to good health.

If you are looking for more great recipes that your whole family will love, including more information on how to implement a healthy lifestyle, please refer to the information on page 188 to order my cookbook, *Preparing Whole Foods for a Whole Month That Your Whole Family Will Enjoy!* May God bless you!

Now may the Lord of peace himself give you peace at all times
and in every way. The Lord be with all of you.
2 Thessalonians 3:16

Chapter 12 Study Questions

1. What are the benefits of making comprehensive health changes versus moderate ones?

   _____

   _____

   _____

2. When choosing food, ask yourself, "Will this food bring_____ or _____?"

3. What Scriptures have most encouraged and motivated you to become healthier? Write them on note cards and place them in key places around your house.

   _____

   _____

   _____

4. What lifestyle changes have you decided to make as a result of this study?

   _____

   _____

   _____

5. Write a simple plan for implementing a healthy lifestyle for yourself or your family.

_____

_____

_____

_____

_____

_____

6. What challenges do you expect as you commit to living a healthy lifestyle? How do you plan to combat them?

_____

_____

_____

_____

_____

_____

_____

_____

7. List some ways you can encourage your husband and children to try and enjoy new healthy foods.

_____

_____

_____

8. List three main reasons you want to make a change to a truly healthy lifestyle.

_____

_____

_____

9. Write out your goals in bold print and post them where you will see them throughout the day. If you haven't already found an accountability partner or friend to encourage you, consider now who you might ask and contact her.

_____

_____

_____

_____

_____

_____

Congratulations on finishing this study! I hope that the Lord has used it to encourage and motivate you to always look to Him in all things, and to choose His best. What the world offers is counterfeit, but what the Lord offers is abundant life through Jesus Christ, both spiritually and physically. May He bless you for your perseverance and desire to fulfill His will. I pray that He will give you His strength, and His will to accomplish His purpose in your life.

Protein from Sample Vegetarian Menu

Protein/grams

Breakfast
Oatmeal 6
Whole Wheat Toast 5
Orange Juice 1.75

Snack
Cantaloupe 1.3

Lunch
Hummus Pockets 12
Spinach Salad 3

Snack
Raspberries 1.48
Almonds 6

Dinner
Lentil-Rice Soup 14
Whole Wheat Bread . . .5
Green Leaf Salad 1.5

Snack
Grapes 1

Total Grams of Protein: 58.03 (see page 65)

USDA National Nutrient Database for Standard Reference, Release 18. Retrieved January 25, 2006, from: www.nal.usda.gov

Tessler, Gordon and Laura. *Cooking for Life*. Raleigh, North Carolina: Be Well Publications, 1995.

Recommended Reading

Food is Your Best Medicine, by Henry G. Beiler, M.D.

Milk: The Deadly Poison, by Robert Cohen

Fit for Life: A New Beginning, The Ultimate Diet and Health Plan, by Harvey Diamond

Disease-Proof Your Child: Good Food for Good Health, by Joel Fuhrman, M.D.

Eat to Live, The Revolutionary Formula for Fast and Sustained Weight Loss, by Joel Fuhrman, M.D.

Fasting and Eating for Health: A Medical Doctor's Program for Conquering Disease, by Joel Fuhrman, M.D.

The McDougall Program for a Healthy Heart, by John McDougall, M.D.

The McDougall Program for Maximum Weight Loss, by John McDougall, M.D.

The McDougall Program—12 Days to Dynamic Health, by John McDougall, M.D.

Juice Fasting and Detoxification: Use the Healing Power of Fresh Juice to Feel Young and Look Great: The Fastest Way to Restore Your Health, by Steve Meyerowitz

Diet for a New America, by John Robbins

Food, Fasting & Faith, by Lester Roloff

Soul, Mind, Body, by Lester Roloff

The Cancer Answer, by Maureen Salaman

Homogenized! Homogenized Milk Exposed, by Nicholas Sampsidis

Common Sense Health and Healing, by Dr. Richard Schultz

173

Healing Colon Disease Naturally, by Dr. Richard Schulze

Healing Liver and Gallbladder Disease Naturally, by Dr. Richard Schulze

Healing Kidney and Bladder Disease Naturally, by Dr. Richard Schulze

There are No Incurable Diseases: Dr. Richard Schulze's 30-Day Intensive Cleansing and Detoxification Program, by Dr. Richard Schulze

The Genesis Diet, by Gordon Tessler, Ph.D.

Chapter Notes

Chapter 2

1. Barker, Kenneth, gen. ed. *The NIV Study Bible*. Grand Rapids, MI: Zondervan Publishing House, 1995. Deuteronomy 30:15, Deuteronomy 28:2, Genesis 49:25, Deuteronomy 5:29, Deuteronomy 5:33.

2. Barker, Kenneth, gen. ed. *The NIV Study Bible*. Grand Rapids, MI: Zondervan Publishing House, 1995. Mark 1:29-45, Mark 2:1-12, Mark 3:1-5, Mark 5:21-43, Mark 7:31-37, Mark 10:46-52.

Chapter 3

1. Barker, Kenneth, gen. ed. *The NIV Study Bible*. Grand Rapids, MI: Zondervan Publishing House, 1995. 2 Peter 1:3.

Chapter 5

1. Colbert, Don, M.D. *What Would Jesus Eat? The Ultimate Program for Eating Well, Feeling Great, and Living Longer*. Tennessee: Thomas Nelson Publishers, 2002.

2. Tessler, Gordon S., Ph.D. *The Genesis Diet*. Raleigh, North Carolina: Be Well Publications, 1996.

3. Malkmus, George H. *God's Way to Ultimate Health, A common sense guide for eliminating sickness through nutrition.* Shelby, North Carolina: Hallelujah Acres Publishing, 2003. p. 97.

Chapter 6

1. Malkmus, George H. *God's Way to Ultimate Health, A common sense guide for eliminating sickness through nutrition.* Shelby, North Carolina: Hallelujah Acres Publishing, 2003. p. 88.

2. Occipini, Mark J., M.S. *Does Milk Really Do the Body Good? Calcium and Protein: A Mixture for Disaster.*

Retrieved July 22, 2004, from:
www.afpafitness.com/articles/milk.htm

3, Malkmus, George H. *God's Way to Ultimate Health, A common sense guide for eliminating sickness through nutrition.* Shelby, North Carolina: Hallelujah Acres Publishing, 2003. p. 88.

4. Fuhrman, Joel, M.D. *Eat to Live, The Revolutionary Formula for Fast and Sustained Weight Loss.* Boston, New York, London: Little, Brown and Company, 2003. p.50.

5. Malkmus, George H. *God's Way to Ultimate Health, A common sense guide for eliminating sickness through nutrition.* Shelby, North Carolina: Hallelujah Acres Publishing, 2003. p. 88.

6. Fuhrman, Joel, M.D. *Eat to Live, The Revolutionary Formula for Fast and Sustained Weight Loss.* Boston, New York, London: Little, Brown and Company, 2003. p. 147.

7. Malkmus, George H. God's Way to Ultimate Health, A common sense guide for eliminating sickness through nutrition. Shelby, North Carolina: Hallelujah Acres Publishing, 2003. p.97.

8. Rhynard, Jill, *Coordinator of Health Promotion. The Complexities of Cholesterol.* (2002-2004). Interior Health Authority. Retrieved July 20, 2004, from: www.interiorhealth.ca/Your+Health/Tips+Articles

9. Fuhrman, Joel, M.D. *Eat to Live, The Revolutionary Formula for Fast and Sustained Weight Loss.* Boston, New York, London: Little, Brown and Company, 2003. pp. 69-79.

10. Fuhrman, Joel, M.D. Eat to Live, *The Revolutionary Formula for Fast and Sustained Weight Loss.* Boston, New York, London: Little, Brown and Company, 2003. pp. 78-80.

11. Fuhrman, Joel, M.D. *Eat to Live, The Revolutionary Formula for Fast and Sustained Weight Loss.* Boston, New York, London: Little, Brown and Company, 2003. p.80.

12. *Got Milk? Get Rid of It. Retrieved* April 14, 2004 from: www.geocities.com/northstarzone/MILK.html

13. Fuhrman, Joel, M.D. *Eat to Live, The Revolutionary Formula for Fast and Sustained Weight Loss.* Boston, New York, London: Little, Brown and Company, 2003. pp. 88-89.

14. Fuhrman, Joel, M.D. *Eat to Live, The Revolutionary Formula for Fast and Sustained Weight Loss.* Boston, New York, London: Little, Brown and Company, 2003. p. 87.

15. Occipini, Mark J., M.S. *Does Milk Really Do the Body Good? Calcium and Protein: A Mixture for Disaster.* Retrieved July 22, 2004, from: www.afpafitness.com/articles/milk.htm

16. *Why Dairy Products Won't Help You Maintain Healthy Bones: Osteoporosis Factfile, Building strong bones and keeping them that way is easier than you may have thought.* Retrieved April 2, 2004, from: www.milksucks.com/osteo.html

17. Fuhrman, Joel, M.D. *Eat to Live, The Revolutionary Formula for Fast and Sustained Weight Loss.* Boston, New York, London: Little, Brown and Company, 2003. p. 87.

18. Fuhrman, Joel, M.D. *Eat to Live, The Revolutionary Formula for Fast and Sustained Weight Loss.* Boston, New York, London: Little, Brown and Company, 2003. p.85.

19. Fuhrman, Joel, M.D. *Eat to Live, The Revolutionary Formula for Fast and Sustained Weight Loss.* Boston, New York, London: Little, Brown and Company, 2003. pp. 129, 130.

20. Fuhrman, Joel, M.D. *Eat to Live, The Revolutionary Formula for Fast and Sustained Weight Loss.* Boston, New York, London: Little, Brown and Company, 2003. p. 139.

21. Fuhrman, Joel, M.D. *Eat to Live, The Revolutionary Formula for Fast and Sustained Weight Loss.* Boston, New York, London: Little, Brown and Company, 2003. p. 139.

22. Malkmus, George H. *God's Way to Ultimate Health, A common sense guide for eliminating sickness through*

nutrition. Shelby, North Carolina: Hallelujah Acres Publishing, 2003. p. 129.

23. Robbins, John. *Diet for a New America, How Your Food Choices Affect Your Health, Happiness, and the Future of Life on Earth. California*: H J Kramer, 1987. p. 177. Data Obtained from the "Nutritive Value of American Foods in Common Units," U.S.D.A. Agriculture Handbook No. 456.

24. *Protein Basics: Where Do You Get Your Protein?* Retrieved June 21, 2004, from: www.vegparadise.com/protein.html

25. Shea, Carolyn. *Ask Audubon*, Retrieved July 27, 2004, from: http:/magazine.audubon.org/ask/ask0001.html

26. Franks, Gene. *Milk Sucks or Bossie's Revenge.* Retrieved April 14, 2004, from: www.purewatergazette.net/milksucks.htm

27. Robbins, John. *Diet for a New America, How Your Food Choices Affect Your Health, Happiness, and the Future of Life on Earth.* California: H J Kramer, 1987. p. 344.

28. Robbins, John. *Diet for a New America, How Your Food Choices Affect Your Health, Happiness, and the Future of Life on Earth.* California: H J Kramer, 1987. p.303.

29. Clean Water and Factory Farms, *Reports and Factsheets: CAFO's Threaten America's Public Health.* Retrieved July 27, 2004, from: www.sierraclub.org/factoryfarms/factsheets/factoryfarms.asp

30. Robbins, John. *Diet for a New America, How Your Food Choices Affect Your Health, Happiness, and the Future of Life on Earth.* California: H J Kramer, 1987. p. 352.

31. Robbins, John. *Diet for a New America, How Your Food Choices Affect Your Health, Happiness, and the Future of Life on Earth.* California: H J Kramer, 1987. p. 351.

32. Robbins, John. *Diet for a New America, How Your Food Choices Affect Your Health, Happiness, and the Future of Life on Earth.* California: H J Kramer, 1987. p. 372.

33. *Meat and the Environment.* Retrieved April 27, 2004, from www.goveg.com/feat/enviro.html,

34. Robbins, John. *Diet for a New America, How Your Food Choices Affect Your Health, Happiness, and the Future of Life on Earth.* California: H J Kramer, 1987. p. 352.

35. Robbins, John. *Diet for a New America, How Your Food Choices Affect Your Health, Happiness, and the Future of Life on Earth.* California: H J Kramer, 1987. p. 134.

36. *Citizens Against Government Waste. Milk Marketing Order Reform: Watered Down or Real?* Retrieved July 12, 2004, from: www.cagw.org/site/PageServer?pagename=reports_milkmarketing

37. *Citizens Against Government Waste. Milk Marketing Order Reform: Watered Down or Real?* Retrieved July 12, 2004, from: www.cagw.org/site/PageServer?pagename=reports_milkmarketing

38. Robbins, John. *Diet for a New America, How Your Food Choices Affect Your Health, Happiness, and the Future of Life on Earth.* California: H J Kramer, 1987. pp.113-114.

39. Robbins, John. *Diet for a New America, How Your Food Choices Affect Your Health, Happiness, and the Future of Life on Earth.* California: H J Kramer, 1987. p. 62.

40. Robbins, John. *Diet for a New America, How Your Food Choices Affect Your Health, Happiness, and the Future of Life on Earth.* California: H J Kramer, 1987. p. 56.

41. Robbins, John. *Diet for a New America, How Your Food Choices Affect Your Health, Happiness, and the Future of Life on Earth.* California: H J Kramer, 1987. p. 54.

42. Robbins, John. *Diet for a New America, How Your Food Choices Affect Your Health, Happiness, and the Future of Life on Earth.* California: H J Kramer, 1987. p.93.

43. Robbins, John. *Diet for a New America, How Your Food Choices Affect Your Health, Happiness, and the Future of Life on Earth.* California: H J Kramer, 1987. p. 84.

44. Robbins, John. *Diet for a New America, How Your Food Choices Affect Your Health, Happiness, and the Future of Life on Earth*. California: H J Kramer, 1987. p.94.

45. Robbins, John. *Diet for a New America, How Your Food Choices Affect Your Health, Happiness, and the Future of Life on Earth*. California: H J Kramer, 1987. p. 367.

46. Robbins, John. *Diet for a New America, How Your Food Choices Affect Your Health, Happiness, and the Future of Life on Earth*. California: H J Kramer, 1987. p. 62.

47. Robbins, John. *Diet for a New America, How Your Food Choices Affect Your Health, Happiness, and the Future of Life on Earth*. California: H J Kramer, 1987. p. 351.

48. Robbins, John. *Diet for a New America, How Your Food Choices Affect Your Health, Happiness, and the Future of Life on Earth*. California: H J Kramer, 1987. p.361.

49. Robbins, John. *Diet for a New America, How Your Food Choices Affect Your Health, Happiness, and the Future of Life on Earth*. California: H J Kramer, 1987. p.352.

50. Robbins, John. *Diet for a New America, How Your Food Choices Affect Your Health, Happiness, and the Future of Life on Earth*. California: H J Kramer, 1987. p.363.

51. Robbins, John. *Diet for a New America, How Your Food Choices Affect Your Health, Happiness, and the Future of Life on Earth*. California: H J Kramer, 1987. p.367.

52. Environment News Service. *Factory Farms Grow New Roots in Developing World*. (April 22, 2003). Retrieved July 27, 2004 from: www.worldrevolution.org/article/857

53. *Clean Water and Factory Farms, Reports and Factsheets: CAFO's Threaten America's Public Health*. Retrieved July 27, 2004, from: www.sierraclub.org/ factoryfarms/factsheets/factoryfarms.asp

54. National Resources Defense Council. *Pollution From Giant Livestock Farms Threatens Public Health*. Retrieved July 27, 2004 from: www.nrdc.org/water/pollution/nspills.asp

55. National Resources Defense Council. *Pollution From Giant Livestock Farms Threatens Public Health.* Retrieved July 27, 2004 from: www.nrdc.org/water/pollution/nspills.asp

56. Robbins, John. *Diet for a New America, How Your Food Choices Affect Your Health, Happiness, and the Future of Life on Earth.* California: H J Kramer, 1987. p.373.

57. Simon, Michele, JD, MPH. *The Politics of Meat and Dairy.* Retrieved April 14, 2004 from: www.earthsave.org/news/polsmd.htm

58. Simon, Michele, JD, MPH. *The Politics of Meat and Dairy.* Retrieved April 14, 2004 from: www.earthsave.org/news/polsmd.htm

59. Farm Service Agency: *Commodity Operations.* Retrieved July 16, 2004, from: www.fsa.usda.gov/daco/default.htm

Chapter 7

1. Fuhrman, Joel, M.D. *Eat to Live, The Revolutionary Formula for Fast and Sustained Weight Loss.* Boston, New York, London: Little, Brown and Company, 2003. p.34.

2. Fuhrman, Joel, M.D. *Eat to Live, The Revolutionary Formula for Fast and Sustained Weight Loss.* Boston, New York, London: Little, Brown and Company, 2003. p. 31.

3. Fuhrman, Joel, M.D. *Eat to Live, The Revolutionary Formula for Fast and Sustained Weight Loss.* Boston, New York, London: Little, Brown and Company, 2003. p.33.

4. Fuhrman, Joel, M.D. *Eat to Live, The Revolutionary Formula for Fast and Sustained Weight Loss.* Boston, New York, London: Little, Brown and Company, 2003. p.31.

5. Fuhrman, Joel, M.D. *Eat to Live, The Revolutionary Formula for Fast and Sustained Weight Loss.* Boston, New York, London: Little, Brown and Company, 2003. p.33.

6. Fuhrman, Joel, M.D. *Eat to Live, The Revolutionary Formula for Fast and Sustained Weight Loss.* Boston, New York, London: Little, Brown and Company, 2003. p.240.

7. Fuhrman, Joel, M.D. *Eat to Live, The Revolutionary Formula for Fast and Sustained Weight Loss.* Boston, New York, London: Little, Brown and Company, 2003. p.240.

8. Appleton, Nancy, Ph.D. *124 Ways Sugar Can Ruin Your Health.* Retrieved June 22, 2004, from: www.mercola.com/article/sugar/dangers_of_sugar.htm

9. Hull, Janet S. *Aspartame Side Effects.* (2002). Retrieved June 23, 2004, from: www.sweetpoison.com/aspartame-side-effects.html

10. Gold, Mark. *Aspartame...the BAD news!* Retrieved June 23, 2004, from: http://aspartamekills.com/symptoms.htm

11. Hull, Janet S. *Aspartame Side Effects.* (2002). Retrieved June 23, 2004, from: www.sweetpoison.com/aspartame-side-effects.html

12. Gold, Mark. *Aspartame...the BAD news!* Retrieved June 23, 2004, from: http://aspartamekills.com/symptoms.htm

13. Mercola, Dr. Joseph. *12 Questions You Need to Have Answered Before You Eat Splenda.* (2004). Retrieved June 23, 2004, from: www.mercola.com/2004/jan/10splenda_questions.htm

14. Mercola, Dr. Joseph. *The Potential Dangers of Sucralose.* Retrieved June 23, 2004, from: www.karlloren.com/Diabetes/p40e.htm

15. *Benefits of Stevia.* Retrieved February 15, 2006, from: www.steviacanada.com

16. *Stevia News, Tips, Information, Frequently Asked Questions.* Retrieved February 15, 2006, from: www.cookingwithstevia.com

17. Fuhrman, Joel, M.D. *Eat to Live, The Revolutionary Formula for Fast and Sustained Weight Loss.* Boston, New York, London: Little, Brown and Company, 2003. p.241.

18. Null, Gary, Ph.D. *Gary Null's Ultimate Lifetime Diet, A Revolutionary All-Natural Program for Losing Weight and Building a Healthy Body.* New York: Broadway Books, 2000. p.149.

Chapter 8

1. Fuhrman, Joel, M.D. *Eat to Live, The Revolutionary Formula for Fast and Sustained Weight Loss.* Boston, New York, London: Little, Brown and Company, 2003. p. 67.
2. Fuhrman, Joel, M.D. *Eat to Live, The Revolutionary Formula for Fast and Sustained Weight Loss.* Boston, New York, London: Little, Brown and Company, 2003. pp.49-50.
3. Fuhrman, Joel, M.D. *Eat to Live, The Revolutionary Formula for Fast and Sustained Weight Loss.* Boston, New York, London: Little, Brown and Company, 2003. p. 146.
4. Fuhrman, Joel, M.D. *Eat to Live, The Revolutionary Formula for Fast and Sustained Weight Loss.* Boston, New York, London: Little, Brown and Company, 2003. p. 146.
5. Fuhrman, Joel, M.D. *Eat to Live, The Revolutionary Formula for Fast and Sustained Weight Loss.* Boston, New York, London: Little, Brown and Company, 2003. p. 147.
6. Fuhrman, Joel, M.D. *Eat to Live, The Revolutionary Formula for Fast and Sustained Weight Loss.* Boston, New York, London: Little, Brown and Company, 2003. p.50.
7. Healthy People 2010: Cancer, Co-Lead Agencies: Centers for Disease Control and Prevention, National Institutes of Health   www.healthypeople.gov/document/html/volume1/03cancer.htm
8. Diamond, Harvey. *Fit for Life: A New Beginning, The Ultimate Diet and Health Plan.* New York: Kensington Publishing Corp., 2000. p.37.
9. Diamond, Harvey. *Fit for Life: A New Beginning, The Ultimate Diet and Health Plan.* New York: Kensington Publishing Corp., 2000. p.95.
10. Diamond, Harvey. *Fit for Life: A New Beginning, The Ultimate Diet and Health Plan.* New York: Kensington Publishing Corp., 2000. p.41.

11. Fuhrman, Joel, M.D. *Eat to Live, The Revolutionary Formula for Fast and Sustained Weight Loss.* Boston, New York, London: Little, Brown and Company, 2003. p.32.

12. American Diabetes Association, National Diabetes Fact Sheet. Retrieved July 23, 2004, from: www.diabetes.org/diabetes-statistics/national-diabetes-fact-sheet.jsp

13. American Diabetes Association, American Diabetes Fact Sheet. Retrieved July 23, 2004, from: www.diabetes.org/diabetes-statistics/national-diabetes-fact-sheet.jsp

14. American Diabetes Association, National Diabetes Fact Sheet. Retrieved July 23, 2004, from: www.diabetes.org/diabetes-statistics/national-diabetes-fact-sheet.jsp

15. Fuhrman, Joel, M.D. *Eat to Live, The Revolutionary Formula for Fast and Sustained Weight Loss.* Boston, New York, London: Little, Brown and Company, 2003. p. 158.

16. Fuhrman, Joel, M.D. *Eat to Live, The Revolutionary Formula for Fast and Sustained Weight Loss.* Boston, New York, London: Little, Brown and Company, 2003. p. 163.

Chapter 9

1. Malkmus, George H. *God's Way to Ultimate Health, A common sense guide for eliminating sickness through nutrition.* Shelby, North Carolina: Hallelujah Acres Publishing, 2003. p. 160.

2. Schultze, Dr. Richard. *The American Botanical Pharmacy Herbal Product Catalog and Natural Healing Manual.* Marina Del Rey, CA: American Botanical Pharmacy, 2003. p. 17.

3. Schultze, Dr. Richard. *The American Botanical Pharmacy Herbal Product Catalog and Natural Healing Manual.* Marina Del Rey, CA: American Botanical Pharmacy, 2003. p.23.

4. Schultze, Dr. Richard. *The American Botanical Pharmacy Herbal Product Catalog and Natural Healing Manual.* Marina Del Rey, CA: American Botanical Pharmacy, 2003. p. 23.

5. Ornish, Dean, M.D. *Eat More, Weigh Less: Dr. Dean Ornish's Life Choice Program for Losing Weight Safely While Eating Abundantly.* New York, New York: Harper Collins, 1997. p.47-48.

6. Ornish, Dean, M.D. *Eat More, Weigh Less: Dr. Dean Ornish's Life Choice Program for Losing Weight Safely While Eating Abundantly.* New York, New York: Harper Collins, 1997. p.48.

7. Diamond, Harvey and Marilyn. *Living Health.* New York, New York: Warner Books, 1987. p.86.

8. Diamond, Harvey and Marilyn. *Living Health.* New York, New York: Warner Books, 1987. p.88.

9. Malkmus, George H. *God's Way to Ultimate Health, A common sense guide for eliminating sickness through nutrition.* Shelby, North Carolina: Hallelujah Acres Publishing, 2003. p. 174.

10. Malkmus, George H. *God's Way to Ultimate Health, A common sense guide for eliminating sickness through nutrition.* Shelby, North Carolina: Hallelujah Acres Publishing, 2003. p. 92.

11. Malkmus, George H. *God's Way to Ultimate Health, A common sense guide for eliminating sickness through nutrition.* Shelby, North Carolina: Hallelujah Acres Publishing, 2003. p. 92.

Chapter 10

1. Fuhrman, Joel, M.D. *Eat to Live, The Revolutionary Formula for Fast and Sustained Weight Loss.* Boston, New York, London: Little, Brown and Company, 2003. p. 5.

2. Fuhrman, Joel, M.D. *Eat to Live, The Revolutionary Formula for Fast and Sustained Weight Loss.* Boston, New York, London: Little, Brown and Company, 2003. p. 15.

3. Fuhrman, Joel, M.D. *Eat to Live, The Revolutionary Formula for Fast and Sustained Weight Loss.* Boston, New York, London: Little, Brown and Company, 2003. p. 15.

4. Fuhrman, Joel, M.D. *Eat to Live, The Revolutionary Formula for Fast and Sustained Weight Loss.* Boston, New York, London: Little, Brown and Company, 2003. p. 91.

5. Fuhrman, Joel, M.D. *Eat to Live, The Revolutionary Formula for Fast and Sustained Weight Loss.* Boston, New York, London: Little, Brown and Company, 2003. p. 16.

6. Fuhrman, Joel, M.D. *Eat to Live, The Revolutionary Formula for Fast and Sustained Weight Loss.* Boston, New York, London: Little, Brown and Company, 2003. p. 25.

7. Fuhrman, Joel, M.D. *Eat to Live, The Revolutionary Formula for Fast and Sustained Weight Loss.* Boston, New York, London: Little, Brown and Company, 2003. p. 7.

8. Fuhrman, Joel, M.D. *Eat to Live, The Revolutionary Formula for Fast and Sustained Weight Loss.* Boston, New York, London: Little, Brown and Company, 2003. p. 25.

9. Fuhrman, Joel, M.D. *Eat to Live, The Revolutionary Formula for Fast and Sustained Weight Loss.* Boston, New York, London: Little, Brown and Company, 2003. p. 24.

10. Fuhrman, Joel, M.D. *Eat to Live, The Revolutionary Formula for Fast and Sustained Weight Loss.* Boston, New York, London: Little, Brown and Company, 2003. p. 46.

11. Null, Gary, Ph.D. *Gary Null's Ultimate Lifetime Diet, A Revolutionary All-Natural Program for Losing Weight and Building a Healthy Body.* New York: Broadway Books, 2000. p. 34-35.

12. Fuhrman, Joel, M.D. *Eat to Live, The Revolutionary Formula for Fast and Sustained Weight Loss.* Boston, New York, London: Little, Brown and Company, 2003. p. 40.

Chapter 11
1. Fuhrman, Joel, M.D. *Eat to Live, The Revolutionary Formula for Fast and Sustained Weight Loss.* Boston, New York, London: Little, Brown and Company, 2003. p. 43.

Chapter 12

1. Ornish, Dean, M.D. *Eat More, Weigh Less: Dr. Dean Ornish's Life Choice Program for Losing Weight Safely While Eating Abundantly.* New York, New York: Harper Collins, 1997.

To request information about scheduling ChristyWade
for speaking engagements, and to order
additional copies of:

- *Becoming Whole: Eating Your Way to Bountiful Health;*
- *Preparing Whole Foods for a Whole Month That Your Whole Family Will Enjoy!;* and
- *Say Goodbye to Harmful Ingredients—Without Reading Labels! Your handy shopping guide for buying safe, brand name foods*

please call (919) 365-6149 or log onto
Christy's website at
www.victoriouslivingph.com.

Books are also available at selected bookstores and can be ordered through www.amazon.com.

More About the Author

Christy Wade is a wife, the mother of four children, a home educator, and resides in Wendell, North Carolina. She was raised near Fredericksburg, Virginia, and graduated from Longwood College in Farmville, Virginia with a Bachelor of Science in Elementary Education. She treasures spending time with her family and friends, playing games with and reading to her children, and creating tasty meals and snacks in the kitchen. Christy particularly enjoys being outdoors: walking, jogging, hiking, water and snow skiing, gardening, and simply enjoying God's beauty. To relax, she loves to sink into a comfy chair with a warm cup of tea and a good book. Christy has a heart for her family, seeks wisdom and truth in Christ, and loves to encourage other women to pursue Him with all their hearts. She accepted Christ as a child, and now makes it her goal to serve Him with everything she has and all that she is.

Having experienced ongoing personal illness and other health issues over many years, Christy sought the truth concerning how food affects our physical bodies. She was absolutely amazed when she realized that most Americans have been deceived, even in our most basic understanding of the relationship between food choices and health.

On her quest, she came to believe that many men, women, and children are suffering from unnecessary sickness and disease as a result of unhealthy food and lifestyle choices. She also discovered that Scripture and science generally agree on which foods and lifestyle choices build a healthy body and which ones tear it down. Christy's passion is to share the truth—that God's Word clearly shows us what brings health and life, and what brings sickness and death. She stresses the importance of serving our Lord with body, soul, and spirit.